A Chaplain Remembers Vietnam

By: Colonel Samuel W. Hopkins, Jr., Ph.D.
4th Battalion 60th Artillery
1967-68

A Chaplain Remembers Vietnam

ISBN 9780615158280
Library of Congress 20021077861
First Edition, 2002
Second Edition, 2007

Published by the SamPat Press
Printed in the United States of America
by Lightning Source, Inc.

Design and layout by Christine Kjosa and Timothy J. Criswell

Edited by Franklin D. Rast

Correspondence and publication requests contact:
SamPat Press
1027 Timothy, Jacksonville, Texas 75766
(903) 586-4488
http://sampatpress.com/

To those who waited for our return,
and especially those who are still waiting.

CONTENTS

FOREWORD

My memoir is not a history book. You should consult other authors like my editor, Don Rast, for information about the social, political, and military issues of the United States involvement in Vietnam. Neither have I tried to compile a complete record of the Army unit in which I served. This story is a retrospective diary of one man's experiences in uniform. My perspective as a faithful believer in God is that with humility and hopefulness we can endure the vagaries of warfare, without minimizing the horrific waste of lives or savage destruction of property that infernal fighting inflicts upon us. The world is full of conflict and tragedy, yet we must find a way to live confidently and joyfully amidst personal and collective suffering. I frequently assure the afflicted that the day of the Lord will surely come, and that justice will ultimately prevail; a certainty in the next life, if not in this world. Consequently, I have learned to celebrate the positive aspects of my tour in Vietnam, while being respectful about the many sacrifices suffered there. Countless soldiers in Vietnam were able to cope effectively with combat, something I hoped I would be able to do too. Such lives are incarnate testimony that in the midst of conflict one can know inner peace, and I salute them all with this book.

The publication of my writings and pictures was prompted by a solicitation for manuscripts by Vietnam veterans from my old Army unit (The National Dusters, Quads & Searchlights Association). These war buddies gave me the motivation to spend the time and energy (two years) it has taken to leave a partial record of where we went and what we did, for posterity and my heirs. When these men learned that I had enough material for a book, they thoughtfully and graciously referred me to prospective publishers, and to the man who became my writing editor. Thank you, Ed Allen, Joe Belardo, Rich-ard Shand, and Red Sigle.

I am deeply indebted to my family and close friends for reading each passage as it was written, and encouraging me to finish the book. Thank you, Don Doggett, Dr. Forrest Fitzhugh, Dr. Burt Gabbert, George Lucas, Dr. Helena McBride, Cecil Smith, Pat Snow, and Jerry Yeaney. My daughter, Christine Kjosa, who does advertising layouts for newspapers, was my chief adviser in laying out my graphics. Don Rast became my writing mentor and publishing promoter, for which I will always be grateful. My wife, Patsy, was very supportive during the six-month expedition I made to San Antonio to research, reflect, and compose my manuscript.

Lastly, I want to thank Jim Criswell, president of Truman Publishing, for accepting a "niche" type book that required tailoring his printing business to the manuscript, rather than amend the copy to fit into a standard format. Not many companies would take a chance on a coffee table top memoir of the Vietnamese War, but he did. I hope your reading of this book will be as pleasant for you as working with Jim and Tim Criswell have been for me.

Sam Hopkins
Jacksonville, Texas

PREFACE

Don Rast is a highly decorated veteran of Vietnam who served as a convoy commander with the 7ᵗʰ Transportation Battalion. He was a distinguished military graduate of the L.S.U. R.O.T.C., and has written extensively about his sobering combat experiences. Like a number of embittered veterans, he views the Vietnam War as having been misguided and mismanaged. After the war he made a serious study of why "our Charlies were not as good as their Charlies." Don is a patriotic American who has no illusions about the futility of war, or the inhumane oppressiveness of communism with its economic and political failures. Yet, like many who have served with honor, he wishes we hadn't gone there, and laments the terrible waste of lives lost during that conflict. All may not share his perspective, but his informative writings confront us with the indisputable truth that we ought to know our history before we ever engage in warfare again.

A HISTORY LESSON

By Don Rast, Editor

The filthy, agonizing, and degrading spectrum of horrors perpetrated during the Vietnam War represents nothing new in human experience. But in several important respects, Vietnam added something different, something darkly brooding, that sets it apart from America's other, more honorable, Twentieth Century wars. First of all, no front lines in Vietnam compared to operations against the North Koreans and Communist Chinese, or the Japanese in World War Two, and the Germans in 1918. The Vietnam War was Western, conventional warfare, fought against an Eastern, unconventional enemy, who decided when and where to fight—and from his own back yard. The United States and its allies outnumbered and outgunned the Viet Cong from the start, but each blow was like a sledgehammer landing on a floating cork. Somehow the cork refused to stay down. Then there was the uncertainty of what Americans were fighting and dying for in that remote underdeveloped area of Southeast Asia. Initially, the general public was convinced it was to stop the spreading of communism, which was a spin-off political theory of the domino effect created during the Eisenhower fifties era. This might have been true from a Western viewpoint during the ongoing Cold War, but to best understand the conflict, it is better to take a look at the Vietnam War from an Eastern perspective.

The Vietnamese people had been struggling for independence for nearly 2,000 years. In 938 A.D., after centuries of Chinese domination, they gloriously drove the invaders from the Red River Delta at the battle of Bach Dang. Under the resulting Ly Dynasty, which was a period of cultural development and prosperity, an independent Vietnam became a reality for almost 900 years. Ly's role as emperor was dominant. He was the father of this emerging "nation-family"—serving as the absolute temporal monarch in whom all power of state resided. His position dictated that he was also the religious head of the realm, acting as intermediary between his subjects and heaven, or enlightenment, so to speak. Then along came the prying missionary actions of Catholics during the Sixteenth Century. Confucian-oriented officials had their misgivings about the new religion. They suspected it as the forerunner of conquest and feared its affect upon the traditional order, which had been the foundation of the state for centuries. These suspicions turned to reality toward the middle of the Nineteenth Century when European nations were establishing power in Asia; especially the British with control of India and Hong Kong. Pressure mounted in France for the government to take over Vietnam under the dubious guise of protecting its Catholic missionaries who were, at times, being persecuted.

In 1858, French forces captured the city of Da Nang, and in July 1861, they took Saigon. Over the next thirty years, it was in this manner that they expanded colonialism throughout Indochina, or what today are Vietnam, Laos and Cambodia. The basic political structure of French Indochina was completed by 1900, with key policy decisions being made in Paris. Cleverly, the French allowed Vietnam's emperor and his mandarin to remain in power, but only as puppets. What followed as a result of this became another important reason why the war in Vietnam became so difficult to grasp from an American viewpoint—and absolutely impossible to win. French rule demoralized the emperor and mandarin, tending to turn them into self-seekers and "yes" men. Minor officials turned to graft or other corrupt methods to supplement their meager incomes. Like the French, they were soon silently hated by the exploited hoi polloi. Absentee ownership grew as large scale agricultural and rubber plantations appeared. Prosperous Vietnamese, mostly Catholic converts, moved into the cities, resulting in more and more of the land being tilled by poor Buddhist peasants who did not own it.

In such an insidious method, Vietnam developed into two distinct classes—a small, elite mandarin upper class residing in splendid villas, contrasted by the masses of dirt-poor peasants working the land for a handful of rice. This highly unbalanced distribution of wealth in the hands of a few aloft Vietnamese set the stage for communism. I might add that in Vietnam, Buddhism is the faith of poor people, and the Viet Cong professed to be the party of the poor. From a peasant's perspective, the Viet Cong were "good ol' boys," wanting everyone to get a "piece of the pie," compared with the corrupt officials and rich elite that squeezed them mercilessly. Incidentally, it was in a rather odd way that Marxism emerged in Vietnam.

Early in the Twentieth Century, numerous anti-French secret societies developed; however, most were loosely organized having no well-defined political objective. In almost all cases, the fiercely independent Vietnamese people (the peasants, that is) wanted to be freed of their colonial French rulers, no matter what system it would take to accomplish this. Enter Nguyen Ai Quoc, leader of the Indochinese Communist Party (Dong Duong Cong San Dang). Formed in Hong Kong in 1930, it united several existing independent communist groups, which remained basically clandestinely inert until the beginning of World War II. When France flaccidly fell to Germany in June of 1940, the Vichy government ceded all of French Indochina to the Japanese. However, the French administration was permitted to remain intact with many lucrative agreements being made between wealthy French interests in Vietnam and the occupying Axis forces. During all this turmoil, the poor peasants were still "hoeing the cotton" in virtual slavery for whoever their "masters" were—good or bad.

Nguyen Ai Quoc quickly became a national political figure in Vietnam, preaching his Eastern wisdom, coupled with communist doctrine, which hand in hand was what the lowly masses yearned to hear—"We will all prosper by sharing." We Westerners would later know him as Ho Chi Minh (Uncle Ho). This Eastern visionary ironically adopted an initial plan of collaboration with all non-communist countries, including the United States and its allies, to broaden his social and political ties. Ho's united front organization was known as the Vietnam Independency League (Viet Nam Doc Lap Dong Minh) or the Viet Minh. One of the first actions of the Viet Minh was to form guerrilla bands under the skillful direction of Vo Nguyen Giap, operating in Vietnamese territory against the Japanese and French. After World War II ended, seeing that negotiations with the returning French for some form of independence for Vietnam was fruitless, the Viet Minh concluded that the only way to achieve an independent Vietnam was through a "war of liberation."

This insurgent war lasted eight years against the colonial French, culminating on May 7, 1954, with the French army being decisively defeated at Dien Bin Phu by Ho's peasant army of guerrilla's. Ironically, the battle was fought conventionally. After the smoke of this great communist victory cleared, the Big-Four (Britain, France,

Russia and the United States) huddled together to discuss these surfacing Indochina problems. An agreement was reached calling for a provisional demarcation line that ran helter-skelter along the 17th parallel. The haughty colonial French parasites were asked to leave (as if they had a choice after their humiliating defeat at Dien Bin Phu.) For details see Bernard Fall's, "Hell In A Very Small Place," for an excellent account of this important battle and the events leading up to it. With the French military forced out of Vietnam, the Viet Minh (Viet Cong) were given 300 days to move out of the South. Overseeing this was an international control commission with members from Canada, India and Poland. After much internal political squabbling, a paper provision was created calling for the holding of general elections throughout Vietnam in 1958.

While the black eyed colonial French were proceeding to relinquish controls and administration to the non-communist Vietnamese with their capitol in Saigon, the atmosphere was much different in Hanoi. It was there that Ho began the total communization of North Vietnam. After this was quickly accomplished, his attention focused on South Vietnam, where effete, money-seeking mandarin leaders were emerging from their various refuges in Paris or elsewhere. Despite the "rules" of the Geneva cease-fire agreement, a well-organized Viet Minh underground was deliberately left behind in newly created South Vietnam. Ho was a peasant at heart, and, I might add no fool when it came to the welfare of his people, which was definitely much different than the Saigon regime that ruled through fear and greed. This underground network formed the nucleus of subsequent Communist insurgency directed more towards the Saigon Government than the peasant in the rice paddies.

Why then, would a big country like the United States want to support and defend such a demonic government? First of all, the United States and Soviet Union during this period of time were engaged in the tensions of the Cold War. So, there was much face-saving on both sides when it came to supporting their contrasting ideologies; Vietnam was certainly the ideal proving ground, with the Communists in the North posed to overthrow the so-called "democracy" of the South. Secondly, for a country rich in natural resources and a highly developed military-industrial complex like the United States, wars stimulate the economy with increased jobs and productivity. "Window-dressing" the reason for being in Vietnam as a crusade against Marxism by our top leaders was morally wrong in retrospect. Now don't jump to the conclusion that those who opposed the war necessarily condoned communist theory; once again, we must look objectively at the facts both from an Eastern and Western perspective. There is an obvious parallelism in the histories of Vietnam and the United States. The United States freed itself from the colonial British just as the Vietnamese won their independence from the French. A great civil war was fought between the South and North in our country with Abraham Lincoln reuniting in victory the opposing sides. Similarly, Ho Chi Minh, like Lincoln, was determined to unite the newly formed South Vietnam with the North.

After the 1954 Geneva Accord splitting Vietnam into two countries, the United States worked quietly behind the scenes to get a piece of the economic action in Southeast Asia under the guise of the Southeast Asia Treaty Organization (SEATO). South Vietnam was included in the treaty as a "protocol state" with the signatories accepting the obligation, if asked by its government, to take action in response to armed attacks or subversive activities. If SEATO had not obligated itself in this manner, the United States could have easily avoided becoming involved in Vietnam's civil war. But this was not so, and President Eisenhower immediately instituted economic aid for the new country, thus beginning active American interest in South Vietnam. With this influx of Western economic and military aid, South Vietnam became more prosperous. This occurred despite penetration of communists in its government agencies, coupled with venomous attacks of agitation and propaganda.

Hanoi, in the North, was shocked that these subversions failed to arouse the common people in South Vietnam.

Ho Chi Minh, as a consequence in the late fifties, decided that military forces would have to be used to subjugate the South. Recruiting for the Viet Cong was stepped up, along with accelerating acts of terrorism. President Ngo Dinh Diem of South Vietnam became a constant target of Communist propaganda by the National Liberation Front (Mat Tran Giai Phong), which called for an overthrow of the "disguised" colonial regime of the United States imperialists and the dictatorial Diem administration. Probably not one American in a hundred-thousand has ever seen or heard the words "Mat Tran Giai Phong." It is poignantly fitting, that in a war when so little was known about our enemy, that we didn't even know his proper name.

In 1960, the guerrilla warfare had intensified to a point of open warfare, with the Viet Cong reinforced by the entire 325th North Vietnamese Regular Army Division. American "advisory forces" had grown to approximately 700 men, but it was apparent that more "assistance" was needed to meet the extended Communist military threat. So it earnestly began with President Kennedy's decision to increase America's commitment to South Vietnam (defacto, the Diem Regime) by pouring more "advisors," pilots, and support personnel into this civil war 12,000 miles away from our shores. South Vietnam was in serious danger of being overthrown by Communist forces in 1961. Approximately sixty-five percent of the country was completely or partially under Viet Cong control. Diem, a left over puppet from French colonial days, was assassinated in November 1963. Shortly thereafter, in August of 1964, the Tonkin Gulf incident occurred allowing President Johnson to request and receive the consent of Congress to use armed forces to protect Southeast Asia. Thus, United States involvement escalated sharply in the coming months, which soon turned into turbulent war-weary years.

It was the longest and most openly opposed war ever

fought by the United States (1957-1975). Public opposition to the Vietnam War was partially the result of on the spot TV news coverage. For the first time, American viewers were able to see for themselves the carnage and cruelty of war. More than half of South Vietnam's entire population was left homeless by this conflict. The United States spent over $150 billion in the fighting attempting to drive the Communists out of the South. There were four times as many bombs dropped on Vietnam as were dropped on Nazi Germany during World War Two. More than 2,700,000 American men and women served in Vietnam. Of this number, 58,132 died (one of every forty-six), 300,000 wounded (one of every nine, of those, 75,000 were permanently disabled). About 1,300 still remain missing. In ironic tribute, United States forces never lost a major battle, but were constantly hobbled by political restrictions and lack of a clear cause as the war dragged on.

Sailors, grunts, gunners, flyers, and medics—all of us bared mental and physical scars from the war. I want to personally say that maybe it was a feeling of guilt for those we knew who fell while we were spared. Surely, whatever the experience presented, many veterans had great difficulty readjusting when they returned home. God knows none of us can ever truly forget that war. There have been many books written by Vietnam veterans revealing these experiences, myself included ("Don's Nam" and "Ghosts In The Wire"). An Army chaplain who served with one of the most highly decorated combat units of the Vietnam War wrote this poignantly honest narrative. This plainspoken book is the story of such an unassuming young chaplain, Sam Hopkins, who served his country with honor during the Vietnam War. Rather than tell about the horrors and often John Wayne bravado that many war narratives depict, he explains in simple everyday language his feelings, doubts, and fears, before, during, and after his Vietnam ordeal. On his behalf, and in recognition of the many chaplains who blessed the lives of our troops in wartime, I commend this book for your reading.

WHAT DID YOU DO IN THE WAR, DADDY?

Vietnam was like a poke in the eye from Marilyn Monroe, blinding pain from a natural beauty that changes the way you see things forever if you let it. Yet, combat was not all blood and guts heroism. For every day of terror, there were weeks and weeks of other exciting experiences. We had some days of hollow boredom too. Hardly anyone ever asks me about what I did during the Vietnam conflict unless they are a fellow veteran who has become aware of my military service there. In an earlier generation, young adult males had to account for their activities when the nation was at war. My generation was criticized for participating in our campaigns, so we learned not to discuss our experiences in public. Vietnam veterans have endured a terrible legacy about an important period in our lives: the war was politically incorrect, and its combatants have an undeserved reputation of being drug-crazed hooligans traumatized by the ordeal. Not me, and not my unit.

Yet within my own family I discovered that my youngest daughter, who was born in 1969 just after I got off active duty, had been quietly curious about my combat experiences. She had respectfully refrained from asking me about the war, fearing that it might resurrect unpleasant flashbacks. If my old unit's veterans group hadn't asked me to compose a memoir for them, Christine might never have known that I have some positive thoughts about Vietnam. Thirty something years later, my memories are preciously vivid about the times, places, and people of a futile war in an exotic land. Many significant things have happened to me since those eventful days in the most exciting year of my life. These days, the photos and colored slides of my all expense paid trip to sunny Southeast Asia are stored in packing boxes. Even though I've forgotten some of the names that were dear to me back then, there are stories and pictures in my head that I often recall in blissful reverie. May the opening and recording of these mental files broaden and balance the perspective about serving in Viet Nam.

When I arrived in Vietnam in 1967, I began to ponder about how a peace-loving guy like me ended up in a place like this. In the fall of 1965, the Methodist Church recruited me to serve a three-year tour of active duty as an Army Chaplain, effective January 1966. Being a Reserve Officer in a holding group, I had been expecting such a call-up for several years. At that time my civilian pastorate was a 170-member church in the little watermelon growing town of Stockdale, Texas, only forty miles southeast of my native home of San Antonio. At age twenty-six, I moved my wife and two children 600 miles westward to Fort Bliss, in El Paso, Texas. The Army assigned me to a newly activated, rapid fire, air defense unit, the 4th Battalion of the 60th Artillery, bound for Vietnam after completion of its combat proficiency training. From June 1966 until February 1967, the unit was stationed on the McGregor Range in the New Mexican desert some 30 miles north of El Paso. Ironically, the men trained among sand dunes for fighting in rice paddies, shooting at aerial targets for marksmanship in repulsing enemy ground attacks. My wife and two children lived in El Paso, while I commuted daily to the billeting and training site of my new "Duster" unit. The unit equipment, twin 40-millimeter guns on a tank like tracked vehicle and quad-.50 caliber machines guns mounted on trucks, were originally designed for defense against low-level aircraft. In Vietnam the guns were employed as ground support, anti-personnel weapons. These weapons had earned the nickname of "dusters" during the Korean War where they had been used to break up the massive human wave attacks of the invading Chinese Army. Their withering firepower kicked up clouds of dust around these ground level targets. The guns could just have easily been called "wood choppers" since they could level forests with one sweep of their blistering steel streams of hot death. The commander of the 4th Battalion 60th Artillery, Lieutenant Colonel William Brandt, welcomed me into his unit, along with 800 other newly assigned officers and enlisted personnel. Our battalion had "E" Battery of the 41st Artillery (quad-.50 machine guns) attached to us for future operations. Later, after arriving in Vietnam, we had a searchlight unit, "B" battery of the 29th Artillery, added to our battalion operations. Specialist Fourth Class (SP4) Robert Bishop, a draftee, was assigned to be my Chaplain's Assistant. When a Bishop is assigned to work for a Chaplain, you know that the Army has a sense of humor. My trusty aid and companion served God and country honorably until completing his two years of obligated service while in Vietnam, returning safely to his home in California.

The 4/60th personnel were a curious combination of grizzly career men and a host of "newbies." A handful of the cadre had served in World War II and the Korean War. Their combat records were impressive and earned my full admiration. I listened to First Sergeant Berry somberly tell about having two tanks shot out from under him when he was in Korea. One warrant officer had been in the liberation of Paris during WW-II, and gleefully recalled how the grateful French women had showered him with affection as they paraded down the Champs Ellysees. I couldn't possibly imagine how they could face going to battle for a third time in their military careers. Other than a little ROTC drill and ceremony in college, I was more like the countless inexperienced draftees who filled the ranks and had to prepare for their first taste of warfare. The enlisted men were about to be led by about twenty-five newly commissioned second lieutenants, who had just graduated from two classes of Officer Candidate School (OCS). Try imagining the humor of watching fifteen men with the same date of rank arguing about who was senior to whom in determining privileges for themselves. Some of the lieutenants had been junior non-commissioned officers (NCOs) before going to OCS, and thought they knew something about the Army. A couple of men had been drafted and were offered OCS after they completed basic training. The unit took at least one nineteen-year-old officer to Vietnam. He was self-conscious about his age amidst the decorated heroes around him. The old timers had started out young too, and were willing to help anyone who had a humble attitude about having a lot to learn.

During this period of rapid build up of units for the war, two sister Duster units, the 5th Battalion 2nd Artillery and the 1st Battalion 44th Artillery, formed up with us at Fort Bliss and quickly shipped over to Vietnam ahead of our unit. The three units got well acquainted with each other while stateside. I especially valued my friendships with the other battalion chaplains, Harland Confer and Arthur Wright. The 4/60th profited from the lessons our predecessors learned in their training and combat. Their experience better prepared us for our own deployment. For instance, after operating in the Third Corps area that included Saigon, the 5/2 Artillery advised us to buy and pack washing machines for doing personal laundry when we arrived "in-country." The unit maintenance section provided us with portable gas powered generators to operate these handy conveniences. Thus, the unit personnel were not so dependent upon the slower Army laundry system or the local economy to get clothes cleaned. The 1/44 Artillery's utilization in the First Corps that included the DMZ (demilitarized zone between North and South Vietnam) made us grateful for our eventual assignment to the Second Corps area. The 1/44 Artillery had become the most heavily decorated artillery unit in Vietnam because of the heavy action they encountered supporting the Marine Corps. After we arrived in Vietnam, we exchanged personnel with the 1/44th as part of an "infusion" system designed to avoid a rotation hump at the end of our tour. The men who transferred out of the 4/60th into the First Corps area entered a highly dangerous war zone, and we worried about their safety there. For the men of the 1/44th transferring into our unit, the Second Corps became their respite from constant rocket attacks and massive ambushes along highways to "headline making" firebases like Khe Sahn and Con Thien.

During my initial assimilation into the unit's training routines, the men frequently asked me if I was authorized to conduct services for their particular religious persuasions. Ecumenically, I was more than willing to conduct an "all faiths" devotional whenever desired or needed. But I tactfully had to explain that I could not conduct Catholic mass or perform Jewish circumcisions. The Chaplains did consult with each other about how to conduct the last rites for Catholics or Jews in emergencies. Under ordinary conditions like McGregor Range back in the states, my religious responsibilities were to conduct Protestant Services every Sunday using a barrack's dayroom that had been converted into a Chapel. In order to accommodate the worships needs of other believers, I arranged for a Catholic Chaplain from Fort Bliss to offer Mass in the McGregor Range chapel. Jewish personnel and other faiths were transported in buses to the main post in El Paso for their respective religious observances. In isolated situations when other clergy were not available, I recruited dedicated laymen to lead prayer meetings for their respective faith groups as needed. Interdenominational cooperation was a military necessity that created fraternal ties only dreamed about in civilian life.

To promote Chapel attendance and unit morale, I arranged several Sunday afternoon bus tours for men who had been to any Chapel service that week. On one trip, the group went to the White Sands National Park, where we learned that the sand is really gypsum. The troops frolicked and rolled on the dunes only to discover that a few of them were allergic to the minerals. They broke out in big red welts. Still, all of the lads enjoyed themselves that day simply because they got to wear civilian clothes away from their military installation. One of the most popular trips was a visit to the historic Spanish missions on the Texas side of the Rio Grande River. What the troops noticed most were the lush crops and green trees growing in the irrigated land along the brown waters of the international river boundary. The men had grown tired of living among sand dunes in the desert. The greenery reminded them of their homes in other places from whence they had been forced to leave as draftees. On another occasion, the Chapel group visited a Mexican orphanage in Juarez with predictable results: the G.I.s' wanted to adopt all of the adorable children. The troops had curiously conflicted attitudes about visiting Mexico. By night they wanted to carouse in the cantinas, looking for cheap whiskey and cheap women; by day they were appalled by the abject poverty that had provided them their nocturnal pleasures.

Without a doubt, the most notable stateside religious event for the 4/60 and the 1/41 was the unit's religious retreat held the weekend before leaving for Vietnam. A Catholic Retreat Center in Las Cruces, New Mexico, hosted 125 of our men overnight in their dorms. The featured speaker was the "All Pro" fullback from the Dallas Cowboys football team, Don Perkins. As a devoted member of the Fellowship of Christian Athletes he accepted our invitation to testify about his faith to inspire young men to lead good clean lives even in combat. Everyone wanted to have his picture taken with Don (including me, and I did). He good-naturedly answered our questions about why his team had lost to the Green Bay Packers in the freezing weather of the NFL championship game. Catholic and Protestant clergy led the men in meditations, devotions, and acts of contrition. The Post Chaplain, Mitch Phillips, who had served under General George S. Patton, Jr., in the European theater of WW-II, was another one of the excellent featured speakers. The old soldier challenged us to be true to our convictions, intertwined amidst a few funny stories with advice about dodging bullets addressed "to whom it may concern." A number of the spiritually revitalized troops volunteered personal testimonies during and after this retreat about how the services had inspired and changed their young lives at such a crucial and critical time.

I used the religious retreat to prepare for my own forthcoming family separation. During breaks between meetings, I quietly went to my dormitory room and composed letters to be sent to my wife and children during the time I would be aboard the troop ship that would take us to Viet Nam. Of course there was no way to get mail off an ocean-going ship until we made a port call at Okinawa, which would be over two weeks into our journey. Wanting my loved ones to receive mail anyway, I left the batch of pre-written letters with a trusted friend at Fort Bliss who mailed one of these envelopes every day to my family. The hardest part of the writing project was thinking up things to say about what life at sea might be like without having been on a ship. With the help of my roommate, a Catholic Chaplain, we manufactured fanciful stories about passing other ships during the night or the sensations of bounding through high waves. Each letter ended with soggy sentiments about loving and missing everybody at home, with assurances that I was OK and would be all right in the days to come.

In the months and weeks before our deployment, I received countless troop requests for assistance with personal problems. Chaplains are virtually the only social welfare-helping agents in most military organizations. One civilian paperback book, published for draftees about Army life, credited chaplains as being the equivalent of political "ward healers." Many of the men needed advice about how to get compassionate reassignments closer to their homes, or obtain hardship discharges out of the Army. Because of the war, approval for these changes was difficult to obtain, although a few of our men did get properly released from the Army.

The Selective Service System had inappropriately inducted a few draftees into our unit. An obvious example of these indiscriminate draft board practices was a draft notice I received while already on combat active duty in Vietnam. The Wilson County draft board in Texas, where I had served the Christ Methodist Church of Stockdale before being activated from the reserves, had picked up my name to draft me even though I was not even registered in their jurisdiction. I wrote back to them explaining that I was a draft exempt clergyman who had previously registered elsewhere in my hometown of San Antonio in Bexar County. To which I added, that I would be glad to come back for a draft board hearing if and when they could arrange transportation for me out of the war zone. Oddly enough, they never saw fit to respond to my reply. In my opinion, the draft lottery, that was instituted several years after our tour of duty, improved the selective service process and eliminated some of the abuses that had affected our unit. In the present era of the "all volunteer Army" the difficulties of the draft decades have almost been forgotten.

Despite these inequities in the draft, the prevailing troop attitude was that "if I have to go to Vietnam, then everybody should go to Vietnam." Correcting the draft board errors was a mildly unpopular practice; nevertheless, upon request, I supplied troops with copies of the applicable Army Regulations and application forms they needed for obtaining releases and transfers. Fortunately, the unit Personnel Warrant Officer, Mr. Robert Elliot, was supportive of these practices even if some of the career cadre suspected that the applicants were just malingerers, malcontents or "draft dodgers."

There was another group of approximately twenty soldiers who had psychiatric problems needing professional assistance. There was no mental hygiene clinic where we were stationed, so they streamed into the Chaplain's office seeking help. My seminary training at Southern Methodist University included elementary Clinical Pastoral Education at the State Hospital in Terrell, Texas, where I had learned the rudiments of diagnosis and therapy. A few of the men were psychotically hallucinating and had to be admitted to the psychiatric ward of the William Beaumont Army Hospital in El Paso. The sanguine battery commanders questioned the advisability of helping these men get out of their patriotic responsibilities. Career soldiers sadly noted the injustice of sending only the fittest men off to die in warfare, while letting the "lame" live safely at home. My best reply, stated crudely, was that the chances for the mentally healthy to survive were improved by eliminating the "weak minded" who would "crack up" in the midst of a battle, jeopardizing unit safety when it ultimately mattered. The complexity of handling these mental health problems motivated me to pursue graduate school training in counseling psychology, later on, when I returned from Vietnam. Thanks to the generous G.I. Bill, I completed doctoral studies at the University of Texas at Austin. I wish I had known in Vietnam what I know now about helping others; then again what I learned then has greatly informed my understandings today.

Some troops came to me about the military punishments they were given for misconduct. I rarely participated in the Article 15 and courts-martial proceedings to plead for clemency in their cases since I tried "to render unto Caesar that which was Caesar's" (Mark 12:17). There was one major exception concerning two men from the unit's Headquarters Battery who were on extended disciplinary restrictions for multiple infractions. They were ineligible for passes or furloughs during the unit's last opportunity for official leave for men to go home and see their families before being deployed to Vietnam. Even their strict First Sergeant felt that these two young men should be granted a pass for visiting their out-of-state families one last time. Naturally, the Chaplain was expected to personally appeal their causes to the battalion commander who was not inclined to make any exceptions about letting the two men leave the base.

Because of their particular record of offenses, the soldiers in question were considered to be risks for going AWOL (absent without leave) and becoming deserters on the eve of shipping out to Vietnam. This was a very serious dilemma for the commander, and for me. Fortunately, the Colonel relented when presented with my proposition that the families might never see these men again. I glibly asked if he wanted to be the one who had to explain to their next of kin why these young boys didn't even get the chance to say goodbye to their families before they died. The "Old Man" said he would agree to grant them passes, but only if the Chaplain would be accountable for their return. If they broke their promises of coming back to the unit, my credibility would have been seriously impaired in getting considerations for other deserving personnel in the future.

A quick deal was made, I offered fervent prayers during their absence, and greatly rejoiced when those young men returned. The fellows were delayed 12-24 hours beyond their deadline because of verified "bad weather", which required a brief extension of their official orders. Colonel Brandt graciously conceded he thought he would never see those two troops again. He congratulated me, thought I was a very lucky man, and was glad that things had worked out so well. I always appreciated how this understanding commander took a chance on me when I may not have known what I was doing. God was gracious to me on that occasion wasn't He.

MCGREGOR RANGE BILLETING

When the 4th Battalion 60th Artillery was activated on 25 June 1967 at Fort Bliss, the unit was billeted on the McGregor Range in New Mexico. After completing unit proficiency training, the troops packed their duffle bags and Prepared for Overseas Movement (P.O.M.).

DUSTERS

The 4/60 Artillery was an AW (automatic weapons) SP (self-propelled) Air Defense Artillery (ADA) unit composed of the M42 "Duster" 40 MM weapons system. The two guns combined were capable of shooting 240 rounds per minute, making them an excellent rapid-fire anti-personnel weapon in Vietnam.

QUAD .50'S

E Battery of the 41st Artillery was attached to the 4/60 Artillery and was composed of anti-aircraft .50 caliber machine guns. Four guns were mounted together with a capable output of 1500 rounds per minute. These rapid-fire weapons made withering anti-personnel armaments, and were in popular demand by grounds troops in Vietnam. The quads were often mounted on the back of deuce-and-half trucks for escorting convoys.

THE MCGREGOR
RANGE CHAPEL

While training in the New Mexican desert of Fort Bliss on the McGregor Range, the men of the 4th Battalion 60th Artillery attended chapel in a converted barracks dedicated for religious programs. After morning services on Sundays, they were taken on afternoon bus tours of the White Sands Park, the Rio Grande Valley and old Spanish missions, an orphanage in Juarez, and a weekend stay at a Catholic Retreat Center in Las Cruces prior to the unit's deployment to Vietnam.

DON PERKINS
RETREAT SPEAKER

Dallas Cowboys fullback Don Perkins of the
Fellowship of Christian Athletes spoke about
faith and morals to the men of the 4/60
Artillery during a religious retreat a week before
overseas deployment.   His inspiring words
were heard in February 1967, at the Catholic
Retreat House in Las Cruces, New Mexico.

SHIPPING OUT

When the 4/60 Artillery completed its extensive combat training, we began packing and preparing for our overseas movement to Vietnam. The vehicles and crated equipment had to be loaded on railcars in El Paso for train transportation to the Oakland Military Terminal in California. This equipment left a month before the main body of personnel. A detachment of maintenance, supply and transportation soldiers accompanied this valuable cargo by land and then by ship to its final destination. Officially, we were not even supposed to discuss that our mission was in Vietnam, but this fact was well known and often shared with our families. In practice, the command could not, or would not, tell us where we would land, or the tactical area for our operations. Shortly before leaving we were given the APO number of our mailing address for release on a need-to-know basis. While personnel were in Vietnam, letters could be sent home without postage by writing "free" on the envelope where the stamp belonged. There would be no excuses for not writing home to reassure loved ones we were safe and well while away from them. Another benefit was a bonus combat pay stipend, and tax-free exemption of our earnings while in the country. If it weren't for the high risks involved, one might have been tempted to profit from the dividends of military service in Vietnam.

While the men were busy wrapping, storing, and lifting heavy shipping containers, my project was to supply each one with a military approved, olive drab, pocket sized Bible for their personal study and devotions. I carefully hand-wrote a dedication and prayer for their safety inside every testament; 800 copies of them were inscribed in this tedious manner. As the men grew more serious and sober minded about the duties they were performing, I mingled among them in their work areas, personally giving them their keepsakes. Some men were truly devout, already carrying their own copies of the scripture; they accepted the issued Bibles because of the special meaning the gifts held for them, considering the time and occasion it was presented. Other men wanted the Bibles because they thought it might protect them, especially if they carried the Good Book on their bodies, whether they read it or not. All the soldiers had heard about some miraculous combat deliverance, when the Bible served as a vest protector by stopping a bullet from killing someone. Whatever their motives for carrying the Word of God, the soul-searching time before battle inspires men to consider the meaning of life and be more receptive to spirituality.

The tense waiting for the 4/60 Artillery departure date hung drearily over us like condemned inmates on death row. All of us wanted "to get it over with", though nobody ever wanted "it" to come at all. But on 12 February 1967, D-Day dawned, and for the next twenty-four hour period haggard drivers were busy busing troops to the El Paso International Airport. Civilian commercial airliners like TWA or Delta flew our unit to the Oakland Military Terminal. We then boarded the USNS Gordon troop ship for the overseas journey. A series of staggered departures flew eight planeloads of soldiers to the West Coast. All troops were in battle dress fatigues and full equipment, despite being mixed in with ordinary civilian passengers on a couple of the flights. Since it was illegal to carry firearms on a commercial aircraft that included civilians, our people wrapped their M-16 rifles in brown paper disguising the guns, pretending to obey the FAA restrictions about having on-board weapons. The guys wrote some pity remarks on these deadly packages, like "To Charlie with Love." The Viet Cong were called VC, and in military phonetic code the words for these letters are "Victor" and "Charlie". Soon the nickname for our enemy became "Charlie," or sometimes we called him "Sir Charles", especially after coming to respect his inexorable fighting abilities.

Before the men boarded their flights, I met with each group and prayed for their welfare, and asked for blessings upon their families during our coming separation. Fearful dependents clung closely to us at the teaming airport terminal, trying to compress a year's intimacy into those last minutes of saying goodbye. My turn came to depart on an early morning flight scheduled several hours before sunrise. The kids were left at home asleep under watchful eyes of a compassionate neighbor. My wife and I waited in the terminal making small talk to calm ourselves, passing time before being ordered to march single file out of the building to the plane parked on the runway. I confidently and affectionately embraced my wife before beginning my walk toward the carrier in a brisk military manner. I passed through the air terminal exit gate door, going from domestic bliss to possible oblivion. My knees buckled beneath me, and my legs wobbled limply, as I laboriously forced myself onward toward the plane. Grasping the staircase railings for support, I lamely climbed up the steps and entered the plan's cabin, weakly seeking my assigned seat. Though never shedding a tear, the suppression of my fears took a terrible toll on me that dark February morning. After strapping myself into a seat, I vainly tried to catch my breath. The stewardesses confessed they had an emotionally difficult time working on outbound flights like this, knowing they were helping send some of us off to our deaths. We didn't want to believe it could happen to us, but danger was on our minds.

After landing in Oakland, we dutifully boarded a gray-painted U.S. Navy troop ship and found our assigned bunks. With my Captain's rank, I was accorded cabin class quarters, consisting of a six-bunk compartment shared with other officers. The cabin was high above the water line and had a porthole for observations. We learned that you do not want to stick your head out of the porthole to look around at things. The people on deck overhead frequently vomit, spit, or throw things overboard that could land kersplat on top of you. We were midship and less subject to the pitching and rolling of a boat at sea. I've never had trouble with motion sickness, so the voyage was a breeze for me. The troops were not so lucky. They were packed closely together down below, all 3000 of them (including 1100 Marines). After practicing several lifeboat drills, we left port in the late afternoon. The USNS Gordon sailed under the Golden Gate Bridge, noticing that the structure was reddish orange in color and not golden at all. The first night went well, but not the next morning. The ocean is more turbulent around the continental shelf, so the first twenty-four hours at sea are always the worst. Awaking early the next morning the troops took their scheduled shifts for eating breakfast in the galley, only to commence throwing up their meal because of seasickness. Ordinary nausea, combined with the nervous anxieties of adjusting to a 600 foot long floating city going to war, debilitated the men mercilessly.

What do you say to comfort a man who is afraid of opening his mouth for fear of spewing undigested food all over you or on himself? While descending the passageways to visit the retching masses, I stepped around men who were slumped against the spiral stairwell railings, too sick to climb any farther on their way to get fresh air on the upper deck. Moving them was out of the question. The galley tables were a mess. Foodstuff was spilled across tabletops, dripping into pools of slop on the floors. The rancid smell was overpowering. The mess area was aptly named. What a mess, indeed! There were no able-bodied cleanup crews who could deal with the very things that were making them get sick. A green-faced sergeant tried to be humorous about what had happened by asserting he liked his breakfast so much that he had gone through it several times that day. Most landlubbers recovered in a few days, but a couple of men including some non-commissioned officers were put in the sick bay, staying there the entire twenty-seven days we were at sea. Those gut-sick men were grateful to set foot on soil again, even if it was in wartime Vietnam.

The tedious shipboard routine was a simple one of eating, sleeping, and finding diversions to pass the time as we floated across the Pacific Ocean. Card games were allowed. Gambling was not. The officers played bridge while the NCOs and enlisted men played pinochle. Movies were shown, and life stories were told. We learned to conserve water while taking showers. The sailors told us to wet down only, turn off the water, lather up with soap, and then rinse off quickly. When we asked the crew how far from land we might be, they would mockingly tell us that we were never more than one mile away from it at any given time; then they would point straight down to the ocean floor and laugh at us. My indolent, playful cabin mates stole and hid some of the Chapel's communion wine from its storage locker. Alcohol is not allowed on naval ships except for medicinal or sacramental purposes. The wine bottles were sensitive controlled items, and quite valuable as contraband. The pranksters kept trying to get unconcerned me to do an inventory of my possessions to discover what was missing. I spoiled their fun with platitudes about loving and trusting others, refusing to check my supplies since I knew they were "such honest men." Their next ploy was to steal a small glass jar from the galley, put a note in it, and throw it out into the ocean. I've often wondered if anybody ever found that message in the bottle.

Not to be outdone by the officers, the mischievous enlisted troops commandeered the ship's plastic shower curtains for kite making material. On Sunday afternoons they had flying contests off the ship's stern, using the breezes generated by the 15-17 knot ship's sailing speed to take the kites high aloft. We became bird watchers too, admiring the wingspreads of the wandering albatrosses that glided overhead before they so gracefully dove into the ship's wake to scoop up garbage out of the churning surf with their hooked beaks. Kite flying and bird watching were peaceful, soul soothing activities onboard ship.

Because of the tedium of waiting for our mission filled destination, the onboard chapel activities were the best-attended events of my entire ecclesiastical career. Daily devotions were crowded with melancholy men sitting in the aisles of an assembly room meant to hold 200 people. We had many more people in attendance than was authorized. Some men came an hour early to get a place in the room before the programs started. The troops loved viewing a life of Christ film series. Our Catholic cohorts stayed after the films to recite rosaries led by SP4 Sam Getzie, who had been approved by his church to fill in as the Catholic lay leader in the absence of a priest. The ship's Captain allowed the chaplains to give evening devotions over the intercom system. He accorded us the privilege of going up on the ship's bridge to use his microphone. The cramped place was blacked out, making it hard to maneuver around the bulky navigation equipment until one's night vision kicked in.

Sundays were a sacred time for conducting formal worship services on the ship's deck. We used a ship's gun turret for a pulpit and a portable PA system to reach the large crowd awaiting an encouraging spiritual word about matters of life and death. There is nothing like a captive audience to inspire preachers to give prodigiously long sermons. No one seemed to get restless standing on the gentling swaying deck with their heads reverently bowed. In fact, nobody minded this extended devotional time at all; if anything, they acted like they wanted more assurance that a higher power was looking out for their well-being.

The only opportunity for a break in the ship's dull routine came when we arrived at the military piers of Naha, Okinawa, having been sixteen long days at sea. On previous voyages by our sister units, the senior ranking troop commander had allowed all his troops to leave the ship on a brief daytime pass while the ship loaded fuel and supplies. Expectations were high about getting to tour and visit such a storied, exotic island. Veterans riled up the troops with South Pacific tales about accommodating Geisha girls who gave back massages by walking on your back. Morale was crushed when the troops were told that they could only go onto the docks to do calisthenics. Seemingly, the commanders were properly concerned about how troops on passes in Naha city could become rowdy drunks, contracting venereal diseases from quick liaisons with local prostitutes. Yet, a handful of senior officers exercised their prerogative, that rank has its privileges, and went to town on an excursion to the PX and no telling what other kind of locales for the afternoon. I never approved of the military's aristocratic system of granting privileges. Good commanders eat what the men eat, sleep where their men sleep, and lead the formations in physical training. Either everyone goes to town, or no one goes to town is my egalitarian attitude; which shows I was an unassimilated civilian when it came to values for the conduct of leaders.

We crossed the International Date Line, and changed our watch settings almost a dozen times during the steady passage through multiple time zones on our momentous trip half way round the world. I somewhat expected to be given the customary Neptunian naval initiation for crossing the date line like I had read about in military annals and popular novels; but that transition time passed uneventfully. A few days from our ETA (estimated time of arrival), we were ordered to exchange our US currency for Military Payment Currency (MPC). Hereafter it would be a courts martial offense to possess green backs. The monetary change over was supposed to keep American dollars from weakening the fragile Vietnamese economy, and help cut down on the black market activities. Some veterans had used this funny money in Korea, and told us about the utility of having different colored bills in different paper sizes for the different dollar denominations, including paper money for coinage too. The three-week cruise was nearly over, and we were ready to get off the ship and begin our nebulous land-based missions.

Our first port anchorage was in early March at Vung Tau on the mouth of the Saigon River. The crew was concerned about VC frogmen swimming under water and attaching mines to the ship's hull. After dark, we were treated to artillery fireworks that made me think a pitched battle was commencing on the beaches and hills ringing the harbor. Later, I learned that the allied artillery fired random rounds each evening to keep the enemy from creeping into nearby friendly base camps (harassment and interdiction, or H&I fire). Vung Tau, sixty miles southwest of Saigon, was actually a pacified area that was being used by the Americans as an in-country R&R area (rest and recuperation). In reality, we were facing only minimal threats our first night off the coast of Vietnam. Nobody told us ahead of time about these things; so we worried a lot, made promises to God, and buckled down for sabotage that never came.

Some Army personnel were off-loaded and dispatched to Vung Tau. Once they left our ship, the USNS Gordon cruised northward along the coastline up to Nha Trang. We anchored there while more troops went ashore. The next stop was the coastal city of Qui Nhon (located in Binh Dinh Province of the Second Corps), my unit's place for deployment. The ship anchored in the harbor a couple of days waiting for the choppy seas to calm down so we could be off loaded. This unforeseen delay was throwing the onboard Marines off schedule, so the crew pulled up anchor and went farther north to Da Nang. The weather was better there, allowing the large Marine contingent aboard ship to go ashore. Those of us left on ship sailed back to Qui Nhon and waited for calmer seas again. The ground swells would not let up, so we were ordered to slide down cargo shoots into a landing craft known as a BARC that came alongside our ship. The chute was like a bucking slide, as troops scooted down it one at a time. I was loaded in the first craft with the Headquarters Battery. The men had on their full fighting gear, although no ammunition had been issued for their weapons. Chaplains are noncombatants by rules of the Geneva Convention, so I carried no weapon, nor needed any bullets – just faith, and plenty of it, under the ominous conditions. The combat troops around me were not as content to hit the beaches unarmed.

SAYING GOODBYE

D-Day came on 12 February 1967, at Fort Bliss, when we had to kiss loved ones goodbye and walk out the door to begin our journey to Vietnam. We smiled to hide our tears and fears, as we began a yearlong separation from the comforts of home.

MARCHING OFF
TO WAR

The men of the 4 Battalion 60 Artillery boarded onto their aircraft at the El Paso International Airport for flights to the Oakland Military Terminal, where they were marshaled onto troop ships for Vietnam.

TROOP SHIP
USNS GORDON

On 12 February 1967, the 4th Battalion 60th Artillery unit flew to Oakland, California, and boarded the USNS Gordon bound for Vietnam. The ship held 3000 men, including 1100 Marines heading for Da Nang. The Pacific crossing took a total of 27 days before the 4/60 was off loaded at Qui Nhon. A number of land loving soldiers became very seasick on the voyage, and were glad they had not joined the Navy.

MESSAGE IN A BOTTLE

Captain Homer Scott and cohorts lobbed a
pilfered bottle, with a message in it, through a
porthole into the blue Pacific Ocean; hoping
that someone, somewhere, someday, would read
the greetings from three bored Vietnam bound
soldiers who playfully passed the time on the
way to their combat destination.

SHIPBOARD
SERVICES

Sunday services were held on the deck of the
USNS Gordon, where hundreds of men crowded
to hear an encouraging Word about how to live
and how to die in Vietnam. Daily devotional
meetings were also filled to capacity in the ships
auditorium. Boredom, seasickness, and anxiety
were the main problems aboard ship.

VUNG TAU

Our troop ship arrived in Vietnam at the port of
Vung Tau. The troops were anxious about
possible attacks by enemy frogmen, and worried
about the nightly artillery H & I (harassment
and interdiction) barrages exploding on the
coastal hillsides. The scenes seem surreal under
the glare of artillery flares, fired to expose
would-be attackers before they could get to
allied positions.

OFF LOADING
TROOPS

Down the cargo chute went the 4/60 Artillery troops. The precarious ground swells in Qui Nhon Bay were too big for the normal departure from a troop ship. After waiting several days for calm waters that never came, unit personnel had to slide down into small landing craft that took them safely ashore.

IN COUNTRY

As our landing craft took us toward the shoreline of Qui Nhon Harbor, we were prepared to storm the beaches like the newsreels showed of the Normandy invasion on D-Day during WW-II. The transport's front end opened, lowering down a ramp for us to charge forward with our assault on the Viet Cong enemies of South Vietnam. To our bewildered surprise, we discovered we had landed next to the recreational beaches of a major port city clearly under allied control. An American G.I. rode past our troop contingent, arrogantly shouting out to us that "he was short," a derisive term that rookies like us would have to endure until our own twelve month tours would hopefully come to an end. "Short timers" were those troops nearing the end of their year in Nam who delighted in gloating about going home before other personnel who had not been in Vietnam as long as they had. We quickly learned that there was an Army Post Exchange only two blocks from our waterfront "combat" position. The unit might as well have landed at Waikiki Beach. As first arrivals, we assured the anxious men who landed after us that they could relax momentarily, since we were not under attack, nor did we expect one in that location. All of us, in one way or another, silently thanked God for such a safe beginning. After this anti-climatic disembarkment, the troops patiently waited for a truck convoy to pick them up and transport the unit thirty miles inland to the perimeter of the Phu Cat Airbase. We were scheduled to set up our first headquarters base camp in dusty abandoned rice paddies ringed with tall bamboo forests. The major disadvantage of fielding a new unit like ours was that none of our people had any prior experience "in country". We had very few mentors to guide us, and sorely suffered from this deficiency in the early hours of our operations.

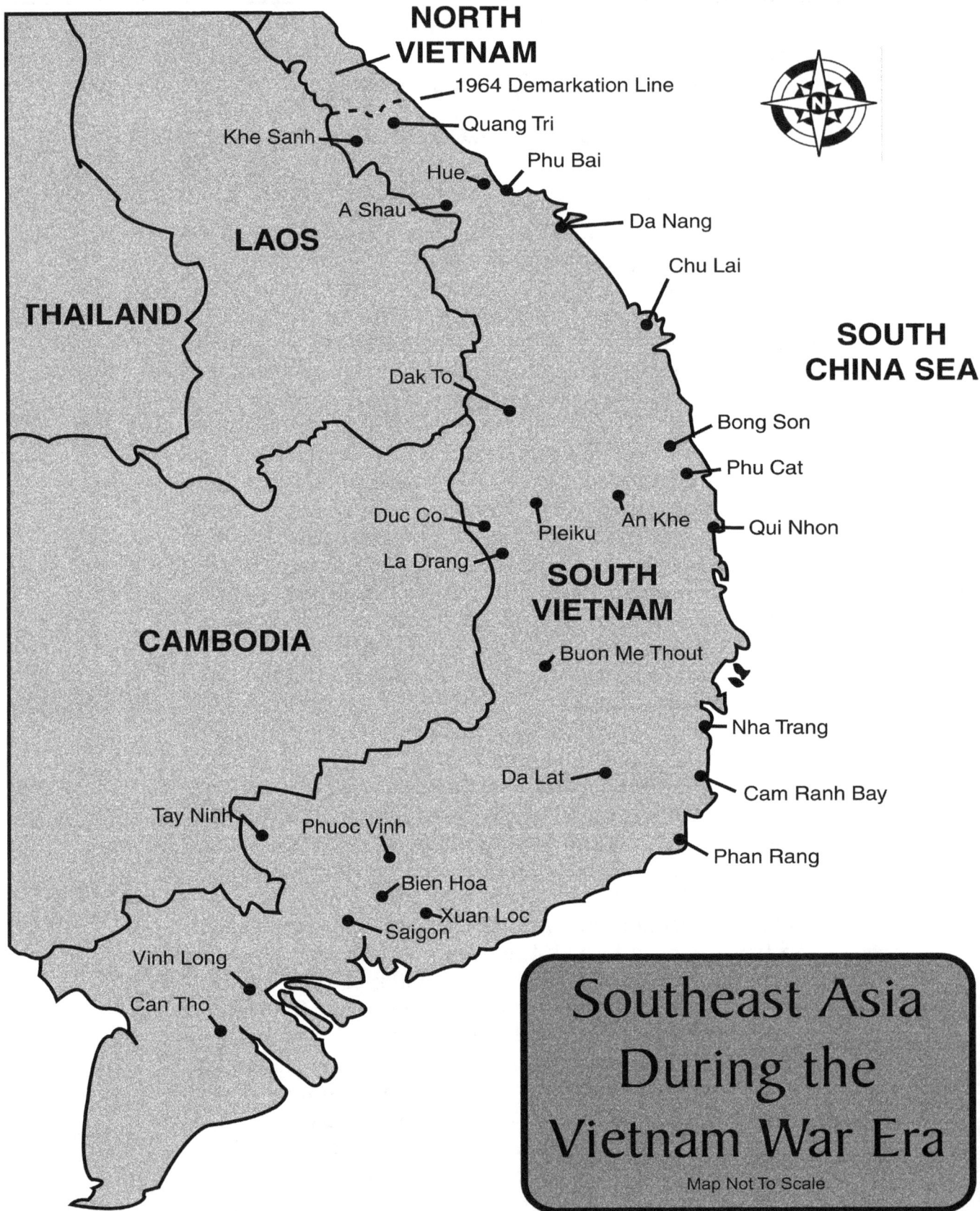

NORTH VIETNAM

1964 Demarkation Line

Quang Tri

Khe Sanh

Hue
Phu Bai

A Shau

Da Nang

Chu Lai

LAOS

THAILAND

Dak To

SOUTH
CHINA SEA

Bong Son

Phu Cat

Duc Co

Pleiku

An Khe

Qui Nhon

La Drang

SOUTH
VIETNAM

CAMBODIA

Buon Me Thout

Nha Trang

Da Lat

Cam Ranh Bay

Tay Ninh

Phuoc Vinh

Phan Rang

Bien Hoa

Xuan Loc

Saigon

Vinh Long

Can Tho

Southeast Asia During the Vietnam War Era

Map Not To Scale

A transportation unit belatedly dispatched some deuce and half trucks (two and half tons) to meet us at the beach and take us inland. An orange glob of setting sun cast its dimming rays upon me as I climbed into the cab of my assigned truck to sit beside a very nervous teen-age driver. A squad of men climbed into the back-end of the truck, and we bumpily took off. The truck's windshield had a bullet hole that had cracked its glass in a spider web design. Our driver alarmingly talked about the threat of receiving sniper fire, as we tensely rode to our unfamiliar destination in the dark. He drove rapidly, double clutching the racing engine, up the infamous Highway One to keep us from being an easy target. We passed by peasant straw huts with dimly lit lanterns, emitting smells of incense and cooking food, wondering who was going to lob a grenade into our midst. To everyone's great relief, no trucks were attacked before we arrived at our prearranged campsite. Our unit had sent an advanced party to survey the location and set up a few tents before the main body arrived. The moonless night was pitch black, so naturally confusion abounded; the troops groped about the area to find their equipment and duffel bags without using flashlights. We cautiously crawled around the grounds trying to find our assigned tents and cots, then tried going to sleep convinced that the enemy might attack at any moment.

We lay in fear on our cots, not knowing where we were or what to expect next. Fatigue induced us to sleep, until nearby loud explosions jolted us awake. A Korean artillery unit was firing nightly H&I (harassment and interdiction) rounds that were landing outside the perimeter of the airbase. Of course we were on their perimeter, making the noise sound up close and personal. My groggy mind thought someone might be under attack. What should I do? Where should I go? There were no sandbag bunkers or foxholes for protection. Therefore, I decided to stay in my sleeping bag until somebody hollered for me to run for cover, or go help the wounded. No one yelled out any alarms, so I put my hands over my ears to block out the noisy cannons and wearily went back to sleep. Once again, no one had told us what to expect. In the first hours and early days of being in country, information was scarce. The men had to hang on by trusting in the Lord until they could become experienced combat veterans.

Morning came on 12 March 1967, and I realized that I was going to celebrate my 28th birthday during the intense work of setting up a base camp. The commanders organized their units for prospective deployments across the Second Corps area. The vehicles and heavy equipment that had been shipped separately on other ships begin to arrive back at the port of Qui Nhon. These bulky, heavy items had to be unloaded and carefully prepared for field duty. Fortunately, we were in the dry season on the coastal side of Vietnam, so the weather was good for these undertakings.

An early Easter season was upon us, and I celebrated Palm Sunday services before a full crowd in the chapel tent. These brave men wanted a comforting blessing before they drove away to unfamiliar places like Bong Song, Pleiku, Tuy Hoa, and lesser-known remote locations. Furnishings for the chapel tent had been made from what is commonly known as field expedient supplies. Empty ammo crates were painted blue with small white crosses on the ends, and used as low standing benches for the congregation. The altar was a wooden table that had been liberated from an abandoned native shrine. An Army issued chaplain's kit provided the altar settings, and hymnbooks were available.

The creative makeshift arrangements attracted the attention of the Headquarters Battery commander, Captain Robert White, a graduate of the outstanding Texas A & M officers training program. He came peeking into the set-up, even though having studiously avoided public worship places up until this time. I assured him that the tent would not fall down if he desired to go inside. Captain White took a few pictures, while commending the place for his men, but stipulated he would not be in my congregation since he only practiced private devotions – or something like that. The man was a good officer, not openly pious but supportive of the role religious faith played in balancing the lives of rough, gruff men under his command.

In appreciation for our protection of their perimeter defense, the Phu Cat Air Force personnel generously offered us use of their radio communication station (MARS), allowing the men to make overseas phone calls back home. Who would have thought that you could phone home in the middle of a war? When my turn came, I learned that the call was relayed through HAM radio operators who could overhear all of the tender remarks being exchanged between separated loved ones. We also had an Armed Forces Radio and TV network to entertain us; that is, if we were located where you could get reception. The morale boosting radio broadcasts by Miss Chris Noel endeared her to the men, as they blissfully dreamed about their stateside girlfriends and wives. Incredibly, the Signal Corp had even set up a television station on a mountain in Qui Nhon. If one had a TV set, you could get popular network programs on channel 11. Many troops actually enjoyed watching TV star Vic Morrow in the action adventure series of our day, "Combat." These amenities made the tour more comfortable than we had ever expected Vietnam could be. The men were elated when they learned that they could get at least one R&R (rest and recuperation) vacation during the year whenever they wanted to schedule it. The good old USA was providing us with lavish logistical support and morale enhancers targeted to offset Vietnam's politically unpopular cause.

During these early weeks of operation, when all elements of the 4/60 Artillery were still at Phu Cat, we didn't have any enemy engagement against the battalion's encampment. Ironically, we were the safest from casualties at the time when we felt the least secure about our self-defense capabilities. However, sanitation and disease soon became a major concern. Some of the men got diarrhea; maybe from the way the food was prepared, or maybe it was the anti-malaria pills we started taking. A few troopers needlessly exposed themselves to hepatitis when they bought some locally bottled sodas from Vietnamese vendors selling their drinks to convoys on the roads in and out of our encampment. In addition, the drinks had been iced down in unpurified water. The battalion surgeon, Captain "Doc" James Anhalt, ordered all the personnel who had bought the sodas to take painful gammaglobulin shots as a prophylactic measure. He just wanted to teach them a good lesson about being careful when eating or drinking goods from the indigenous economy. The men had to cleanse the scratches and nicks they got on their hands and faces to prevent infections. The tropical climate made everything grow, especially sore producing fungi. Initially, everyone was motivated to be cautious about everything. The longer we stayed in country, the more relaxed one became about his health and safety - including the wearing of hot flak jackets and taking of anti-malaria pills. Most men would get very cautious again when they edged closer to the end of their tours, but that was far off in our future at this early stage of the deadly game of trying to survive in a hostile environment.

After all firing batteries convoyed across the region to their initial assignment areas, the 4/60 Artillery battalion headquarters received news of our first engagement in combat. One battery had moved up Highway One to join the First Cavalry Airmobile Division's area of operation (AO) in Bong Son. A platoon leader and a section of his dusters (twin 40 MM guns) had gone out with a small sized infantry unit to set up a position in the An Lo River Valley. They rolled into positions during the late afternoon, camping on top of a knoll. There was no time to fortify positions with barbed wire or bunkers. The infantry officer on the scene was nervous about being exposed to an attack, but neither the Viet Cong nor the First Cavalry had never seen the potent firepower of a duster unit in action. As our standard tactics required, the tracked duster vehicles changed their defensive positions on the perimeter after dark, so that the enemy would not know where to find them. The VC did not wait long before they savagely attacked the American troops, only to be devastated by the duster's withering fire of 240 rounds per minute of high explosive shells aimed lethally at point blank range. Their attack was smashed quickly and brutally. The VC learned a painful lesson that first night opposite our guns, and thereafter they avoided such engagements against dusters whenever possible. The duster crews became instant heroes and were given decorations on the spot by the First Cavalry Division's commander. Needless to say, the infantry slept better at night when they could get dusters to cover their positions.

My first visitation to the forty-two separate locations employing our unit's duster crews and quad .50 caliber machine guns was to the site of this initial battle. No one on our side had been hurt, and everyone was enjoying the victory. We offered prayers of thanksgiving, and wondered if our engagements would always have such happy endings. In a later encounter in the same Bong Son area of operations (AO), some crews went out with the infantry toward the coastline and had a furious firefight. Our dusters came back with armor piercing bullets stuck all over the vehicles' chassis, looking like they had fallen into a cactus patch. The men had had some close calls, but lived to talk about them. Part of my job was listening to their stories and remembering them for the benefit of others. Assuring the hopes and fears of young men in combat is a full time job, and I regretted that I could not be there each and every time they were attacked. At least I could pray for them when we were absent from one another, and the men seemed to value those intercessions.

LANDING AT QUI NHON

On 11 March 1967, the Headquarters Battery
was the first to board a BARC landing craft and
land on the beaches of Qui Nhon. The men
were anxious to set foot in country, and
wondered what might be waiting for them there.
The troops were picked up by a truck convoy at
the port, then taken thirty miles inland to camp
and set up positions outside the perimeter of
the Phu Cat Airbase.

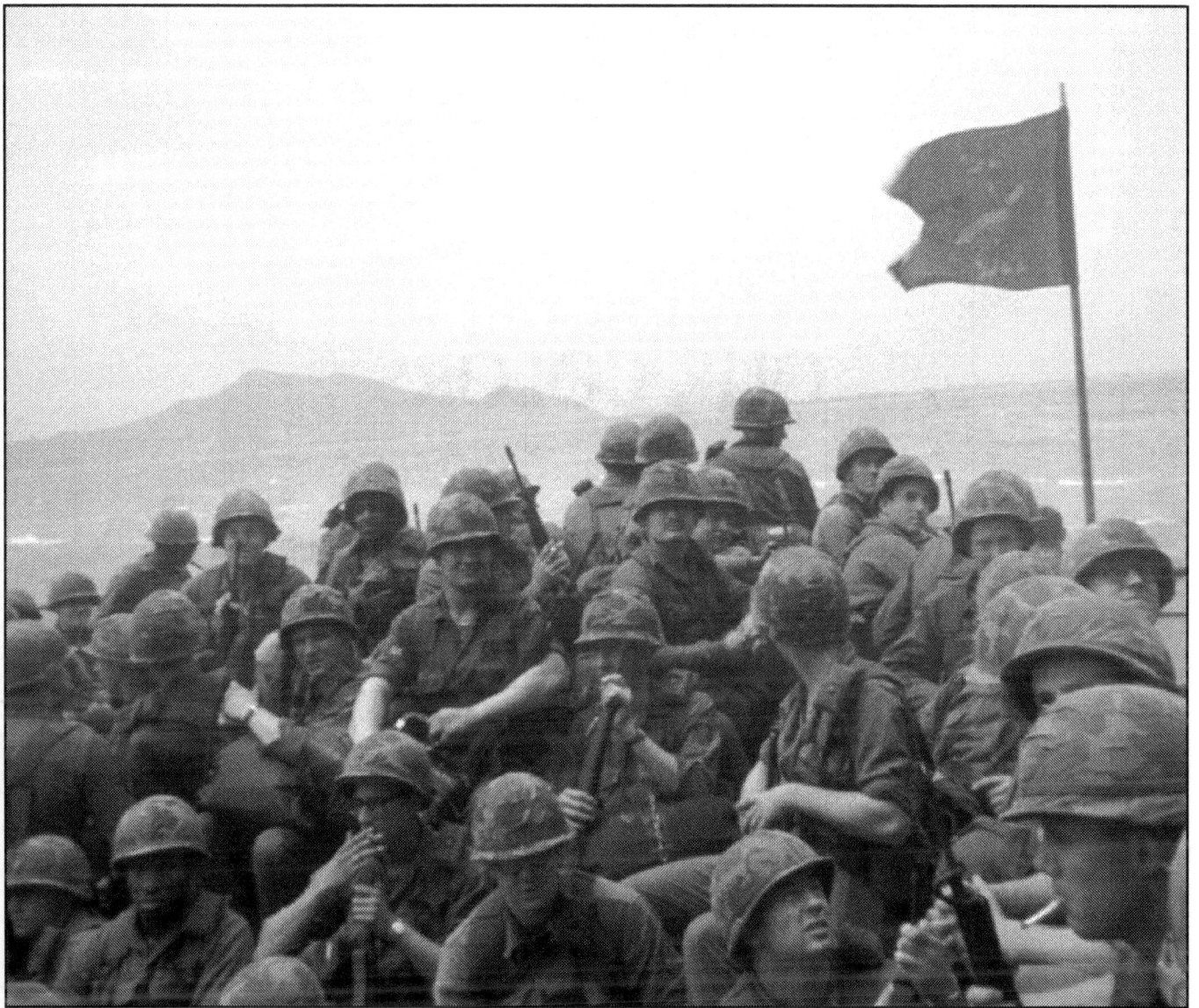

OUR COLORS

The troops proudly unfurled the American flag
and their unit colors as they made camp and
began their combat operations.

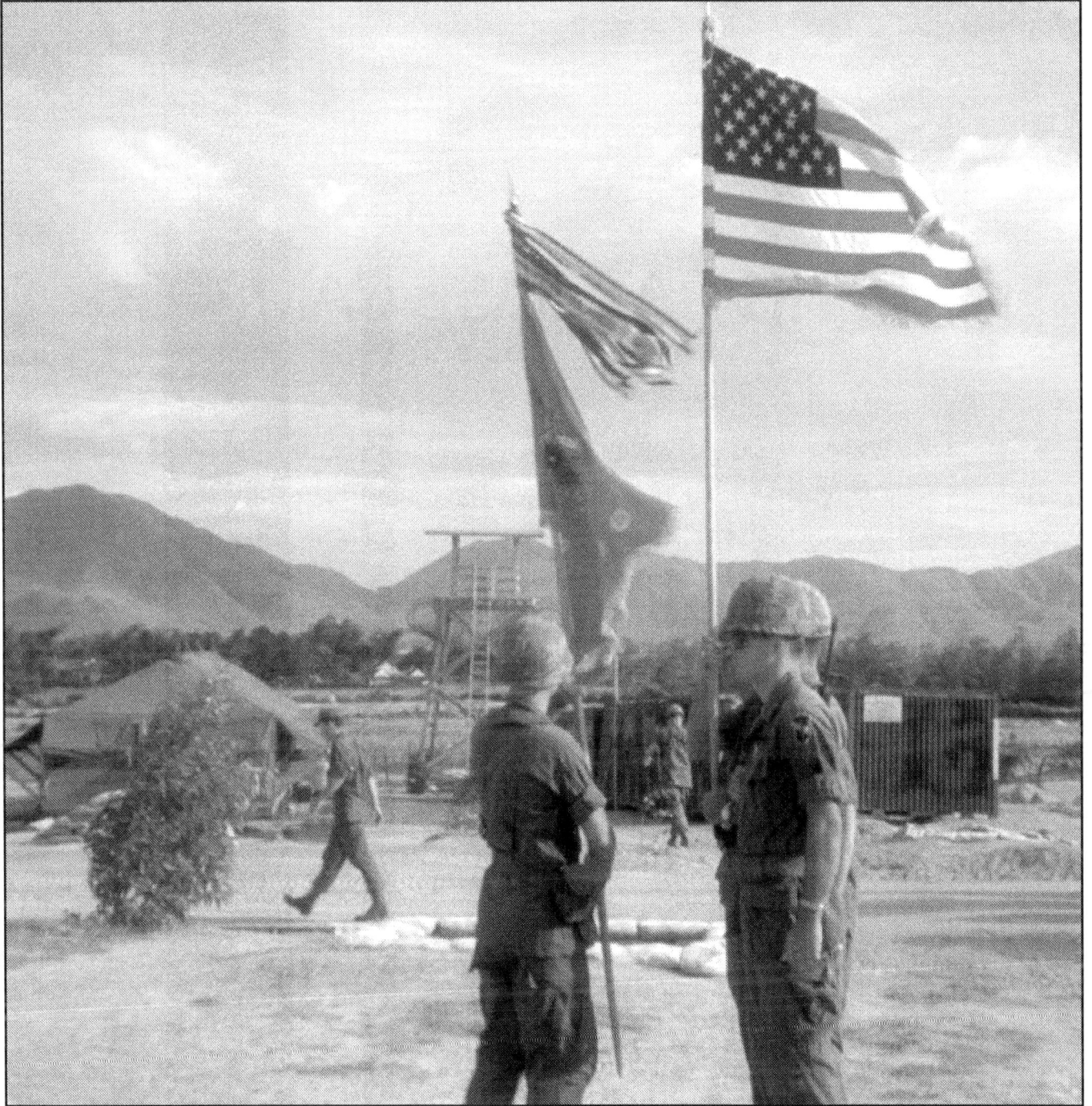

PHU CAT BASE CAMP

The 4/60 Arty was convoyed inland from Qui Nhon to set up their first base camp on the perimeter of the Phu Cat Airbase. The full battalion lived in a tent city awaiting the arrival of their equipment. As the batteries got their deployment assignments, they left from Phu Cat for places like Pleiku, Bong Son, and Tuy Hoa. When they were gone, the Battalion HQ was relocated to Camp Townes near Qui Nhon.

PHU CAT CHAPEL

The 4/60ᵗʰ Artillery set up their first base camp
on the perimeter of the Phu Cat airbase. The
Chapel was set up in a GP (general purpose)
Medium tent. Ammunition crates were made
into low bench pews, and an abandoned table
was painted white to serve as the altar. The
first services were held on Palm Sunday, 1967.
Notice the trench dug by the side of the Chapel
to be used in case of a mortar attack.

FIELD SHOWER AND LAUNDRY

Soldiers in the field are constantly told to improve their positions. In one base camp, the 4/60 Artillery troops built a cold-water shower out of a 50-gallon barrel mounted on a lumber framework. The unit brought stateside washing machines with their unit equipment, running them with small generators. Men who had bathed out of their helmets, or used small canvas bag showerheads out in the boonies, considered these amenities to be a luxury.

HOME
IMPROVEMENTS

After the unit got settled in its base camp, the supply and maintenance sections gradually improved the living and working facilities for the men. The tents were given a wooden floor and screened-in sidings. The next step was to put sandbags around the lower part of the structure for protection against shrapnel if attacked.

THE AN LO VALLEY
A DEADLY BEAUTY

The beauty of the countryside hid a deadly menace. Guerilla fighters hid in the thick forests by day, attacking villages and defense forces by night. The 4/60 Artillery unit's first significant combat occurred in this sector.

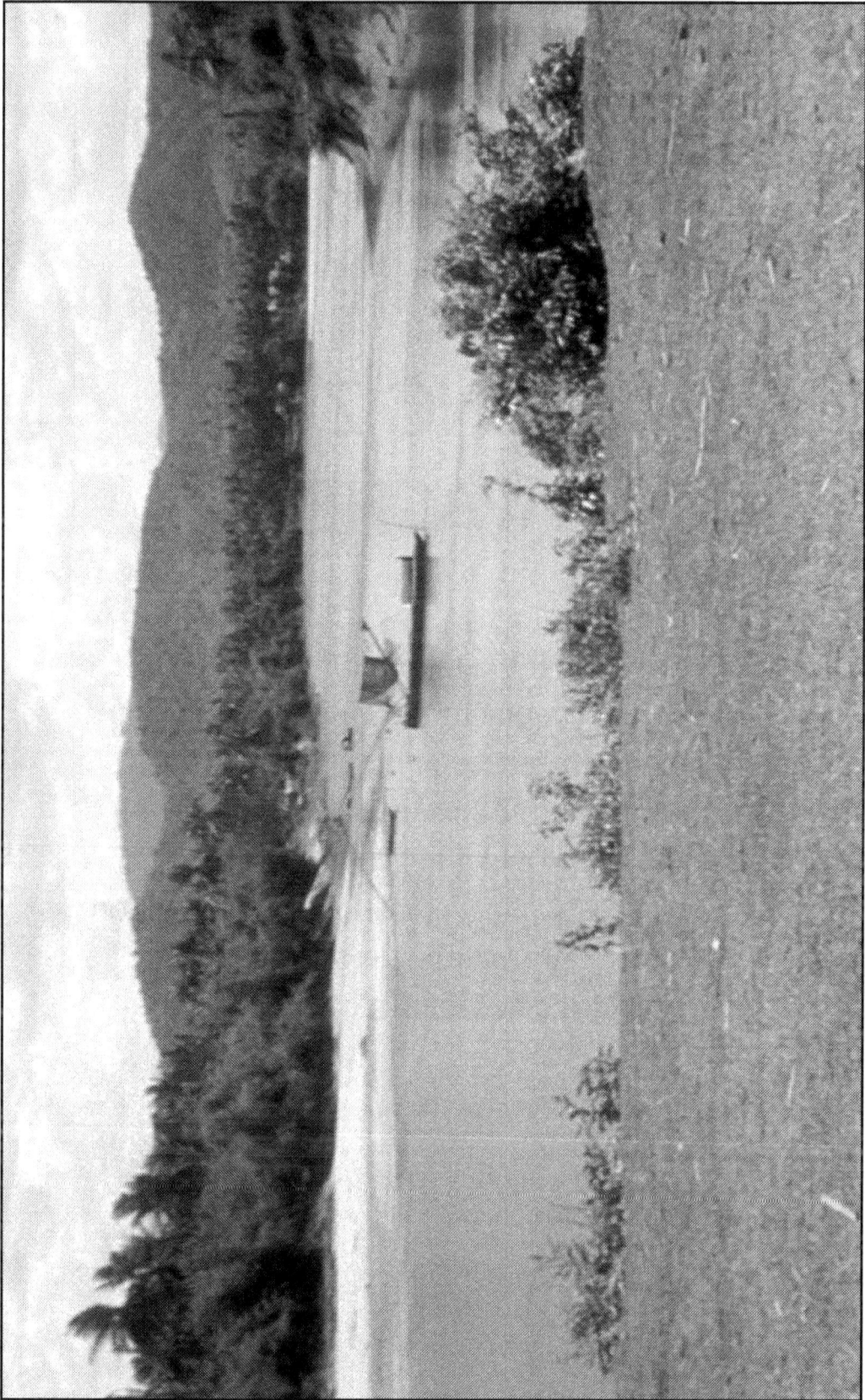

LANDING ZONE APACHE

The men of the 4th Battalion 60th Artillery Duster Unit provided perimeter defense for the Infantry troops at LZ Apache in the II Corps Area of Vietnam. A purple smoke grenade was set off, signaling an incoming helicopter where to land and pick up a contingent of troops going out on a mission. Army airmoble operations were perfected in Vietnam campaigns.

BEACHHEAD

American forces landed a task force in hostile
territories on the far north coastline of the
Second Corps area. Duster and Quad .50
elements were part of this operation. Chaplains
were airlifted in and out of the beachfront
throughout the engagement.

BROKEN BRIDGE

The Viet Cong blew up the highway bridges to disrupt commerce and transportation in the country. The duster units often deployed weapons sections to defend critical points in the country to prevent the demolition of these vita links in the infrastructure.

DAMAGED TOWER

How pitiful that war damages even peaceful old
towers caught in the combat zone. As time and
material permitted, the U.S. forces attempted
some modest reconstruction of landmarks such
as this one.

74

GUARDING A P.O.W.

SP4 Baldwin of Battery C, 4/60 Arty, guarded a captured Viet Cong at LZ Two Bits in the Bong Son area of operations with the First Cavalry Airmoble Division. POW's were not usually interned in tactical unit areas. While "Charlie" was with us, he performed useful labor as a K.P. (kitchen police).

VIET CONG DETAINEES

Four suspected Viet Cong were captured and detained by the South Vietnamese Army. The prisoners were being transferred to a secure holding camp.

THE CIRCUIT RIDER

The 4/60th Artillery Battalion was assigned to the First Field Forces Corps Artillery, who had seen fit to divide up our unit and spread us out over the entire Second Corps, the largest area of the four corps in the country. When visiting the various detachments in a given sector, I usually rode in my jeep making frequent stops at each of our troop positions. At these locations I would typically address a five-man crew of mixed faiths giving the young men some gossip, and then the gospel. Our troops being somewhat isolated from each other, were always interested in what was happening to their comrades across the countryside. I collected various versions of what life had been like since last visiting in their sector so I could pass this "skinny" (gossip) on to the next location.

At each stop, my driver would distribute sundry comfort items and paperback books. An informal pulp fiction lending library program developed as a result of these impromptu visits. When the chitchatting was done, I would lead a simple devotional service for everyone. A prayer, some scripture, then a meditation, and a closing blessing were the liturgical order of the day. After these informal services, I would linger awhile to conduct pastoral counseling with all individuals who had personal concerns. Some requests were simple ones, while other issues were quite serious and even critical. After saying and doing what could be done on the spot, I would bid the men farewell and promise to return in a month or six weeks – since it took that long to cover the forty-two various locations of our unit. During these troop visitations, I saw lots of scenic and historical places, while meeting many interesting souls along the way. Like my Methodist circuit riding forefathers who evangelized the settlements on the American frontier, I made my appointed rounds, then started back to see them all over again.

One combat hardened crew I visited had adopted a stray Vietnamese dog as their mascot. The little puppy had red fur and looked like a miniature chow breed mutt. All troops had been discouraged from keeping indigenous animals to avoid infection from foreign diseases and rabies. This cute little fellow ate scraps from C-ration cans and lapped canteen water from mess kit cups. When I reached out my hand to pet the friendly canine, he licked my fingers lovingly. A mascot was good for morale. No one had the heart to report the crew for this minor violation of military discipline, much less suggest that they should get rid of their fluffy companion. Those stalwart crewmen won my complete support for their little deception when they told me that the name of their dog was "Sunday." Thinking that the name might be a sign of some religious convictions, I asked them how they had chosen such a swell name for their pet. The tough guys smiled, while explaining that they had not seen any Sundays since they had been in Vietnam, then exclaimed now they had one. Those tired troops were never given any days off, and had just found a pleasant way to compensate for it that certainly had my approval.

Farther down the road another hardy working crew had some unwanted animals in their sandbag bunker that were more than just a nuisance. Large rats had invaded their living area and were chewing up clothing and foodstuffs. The vexing varmints scampered across cots, disturbing sleeping men attempting to rest from their portion of the continuous defensive watch being kept over the position they were guarding with their big guns. Our ingenious G.I.s bought some "eradication tools" from Montagnard tribesmen who were selling small crossbow guns used for hunting. The troops mounted the crossbows on top of long flashlights and became sportsmen.

Industrious sharpshooters often displayed rat pelts as proof of their marksmanship, making a game out of their fight for safety and sanitation. Interiors of the bunkers had become entertaining silent shooting galleries, where foot long sharpened bamboo shafts were shot into the walls of canvas sandbags at fleeting targets of opportunity. I remembered a Bill Mauldin cartoon from WW-II about "Willie and Joe" aiming a pistol at a rat in their foxhole. Joe told Willie "be sure to shoot to kill" because he had heard that "they charge when they are wounded." The vagaries of a soldier's life gave us a kinship with the men and women who had served in uniform before us, just as it would with our successors.

One reason those inexorable rats were attracted to the bunkers was that fresh fruit, sundry snacks, and even steaks were in plentiful supply to troops along the main transportation routes of the country. As the convoys of rations trucks rolled past the check points where the duster crews and machinegun crews were posted, good-natured drivers would toss out packages of their cargos to our guys by the side of the road. The U.S. logistical command ensured that our forces never lacked for anything, from beans to bullets. The pentagon bragged, for the first time in American military history, that there had not been one single engagement that had been endangered for lack of ammunition, petroleum products, or equipment.

Some soldiers exploited the lavish material support being sent to us. One of our duster crews was stationed on the docks in Qui Nhon where it was commonly known that the Army's accounting system allowed up to a 10% pilferage loss of everything shipped into the port. Dockworkers were virtually expected to take small samples of goodies for their efforts. Crates of frozen steaks became valuable trading commodities. TV sets bound for the Post Exchange and other valuable goods were taken for use in a barter economy, that on some levels constituted grand larceny and fraud. Eventually some perpetrators of these countrywide crimes would be indicted as the activities of an organized khaki mafia, including the man who became highest-ranking noncommissioned officer in the service, the Sergeant Major of the Army. Some things I wish I had not come across in my travels.

And there were some places that I wish I had not crossed during these excursions. My worst blunder occurred on a visit back to the Phu Cat Air Base, where some of our crews had been left to protect the humongous jet runways. The sprawling base had expanded rapidly in the summer of 1967 after we had shifted our HQ to Camp Townes near Qui Nhon. My driver and I were confused by the many changes in construction. The familiar route from the entrance of the base out to our tracked vehicles standing guard on the base perimeter had been eliminated. We could see our people, but a giant double apron runway lay between our objective and us. We drove alongside the length of the super wide airstrip until I noticed a crossroad running between the two parallel runways. A truck was parked on this road in an open space between the two rivers of concrete. Seeing the vehicle led me to believe that this might be an avenue for ground traffic to get from one side of the airstrip to the other side of the runway. My driver looked both ways to make sure there were no aircraft landing or taking off around us, and drove quickly across the runways to the perimeter fence seeking our buddies. Before he could come to a stop, sirens and alarms went off, as the Air Police came charging towards our vehicle to arrest us. The APs informed us that we had severely violated base security and had endangered our lives by driving across the runways. I pleaded ignorance, apologized profusely, and explained how we had misperceived the situation. We deservedly got chastised, were given a warning, and then were allowed to go visit our unit members. My genuine shame and obvious embarrassment probably got us excused from legal charges.

Curiously enough, my driver and I had to deal with the Phu Cat AP's on another occasion while on their base. After having visited our crews as planned, we stopped at the Base Exchange (BX) to buy some small necessity items. We parked our jeep in front of the building and were shopping inside no more than twenty minutes. When we came back outside to leave, the jeep was gone. Frantically, we looked around the area, but our vehicle was nowhere to be found. Worry set in quickly. Although car thieves had never bothered the rolling stock from my battalion motor pool, many units had resorted to securing their vehicles by locking the steering wheels with heavy chains to keep rival units from stealing these valuable assets. Some pirating outfits went to great lengths to capture unsecured jeeps and trucks, even going so far as airlifting them away using helicopters known as flying cranes. Civilians usually do not realize that jeeps don't require keys to start their ignitions. You just reach on the dash and turn on a starting lever to begin driving, which was apparently what someone had done to us that dreadful day. As the officer accountable for this property, I could be made to pay for the missing equipment; and I was sure to be scolded for carelessness, or worse.

Recognizing the seriousness of the situation, I called the Air Force Police to report the missing jeep. We glumly gave them the unit bumper number painted on the front and back of it, without much expectation that we would ever see the jeep again. To my great surprise, within a half-hour, the APs found my jeep on the other side of the Base and returned it to me. Someone had decided to catch a ride at our expense to get back to his duty area away from the BX. When they were done with our jeep, they parked it so it could be found, and went on about their business as if no harm had been done. Had I found out who was the guilty party, I might have wished them some harm at that moment. My vexation passed by the time we got back on the highway heading back to our HQ. I even began to laugh about the scare we had just endured, but wasn't sure that I wanted to confess what had happened to us that day. We took some good-natured teasing about being caught shopping at the BX, which was all that was said about the incident. Our motor pool never did put chains on the jeep to keep that from happening again. Thereafter, I prayed that the Lord would deliver us from our friends as much as our enemies.

My problems at the Phu Cat Airbase were more than offset there by one of the most pleasurable and inspirational events of my entire career. In December 1967, I had the privilege of attending the Bob Hope USO Christmas Show when he appeared at the airbase on his annual holiday entertainment tour. Troops came from miles and miles around the vicinity of Phu Cat to see and hear this classic performance. Thousands of us came early and sat on the grounds to catch a glimpse of this great American icon and his troupe. His monologue, skits, and parade of pretty girls gave homesick troops a respite from the drudgery of war. We laughed at his jokes, we cheered for the dancers, and we cried when Mister Hope had us sing "Silent Night" at the close of the program. To this day I get very sentimental when I think about what he did for us then. The year after I returned from Viet Nam, I accidentally met Bob Hope in the lobby of a Dallas convention center while attending a Chaplains' dinner. Texas Governor John Connelly was escorting him to some other function. As Mr. Hope passed by us, we greeted and saluted him with all the respect we might have given to the Pope or the President of the United States. He acknowledged us with a handsome stage smile while saying "hello men," proving you can conquer American soldiers with just a little good will and kindness. Bob Hope will make heaven a happier place when he plays his act for Saint Peter. May God always bless this great patriotic entertainer with appreciative audiences like he enjoyed with the multitudes of service personnel who have adored him and his act since WW-II to Operation Desert Storm.

There were other less talented entertainers who toured the country. If there was money to be made, then there were opportunistic people who would hustle a buck if they were allowed into the country. I once heard an off-key Korean musical group play at the Replacement Depot in Cam Ranh Bay. They had memorized the English lyrics to popular songs that they sang without comprehension. In any civilian setting, they would have been lucky to get a booking. In Viet Nam they were a hit and in demand. The men had a bigger demand for the female strippers who enflamed the unbridled passions of frustrated men shouting for them to do their bump and grinds. One component of my unit hired a burlesque queen to strut her stuff for them at their compound. The troops tried to cajole me into watching the show with them. I wisely declined, knowing full well that the naked lady would end up dancing in front of my face to make me blush for the amusement of the hooting crowd. Plans for such lascivious entrapment deserved showers of fire and brimstone, or at least a swarm of bloodthirsty mosquitoes looking for bare skin.

Occasionally I had to use other means of transportation than my jeep to reach our troops who were in remote firebases. We had access to Army Aviation to get us to distant or difficult troop positions. If a unit owned its own helicopters, then finding a ride was easy. Typically though, I had to rely upon the kindness of strangers for my airborne hitchhiking. The large Army base camps had an aviation operations tent/building or assembly area, where passengers could "catch a hop" on a space available basis to wherever the chopper or airplane was going. Waiting for flights for my particular destination could take hours, since there were no prescribed flight schedules. The routine was a bit like the carefree life of a hobo living on the road. After flying to some distant location, I would get a ride to the unit I was visiting; or I would catch another local flight on a helicopter out to a hilltop or a river valley to see crews here and there. All I had to do was pack my shaving kit, a change of clothes, and my portable Chaplain's altar kit. Each trip became a mini-adventure in self-reliance and resourcefulness, and I began to enjoy the travel process as much as the congenial welcomes I received from my drop-in visits.

On one of my trips to the coastal town of Phan Thiet, I had an unusual return trip aboard a two-seat Air Force O-2 aircraft. The condition for taking this flight was agreeing to sit behind the pilot and drop psychological warfare leaflets out of the plane on the way to our next stop. You get to be real flexible about such things when you are a hitchhiking chaplain. The leaflets were surrender passes for the Viet Cong to use, with reminders about the terrible threats of B-52 bombing runs that were designed to induce defections from the fighting. On another road trip, the inclement weather had curtailed flights from the firebase where I had landed. The local unit suggested that I catch a ride with a five-ton truck in a convoy that was heading to my next destination. The truck cab was full, so the drivers suggested that I ride in the back where they were carrying a load of sleeping bags to be exchanged and cleaned at a laundry. The bags were in a large metal CONEX container, so I was encouraged to curl up in soft comfort inside the container as we bounced helter-skelter down the pot-holed road. The trip became so rough that the large container shifted around on the back bed of the truck until I became locked inside it among the bedrolls. The container was pinned against the side of the truck so that I could not get out of the opening from the storage area where I was nesting. When the truck stopped, I had to bang on the metal walls to get someone to release me from the container. No harm was done, since I'm not afraid of closed in spaces, and proceeded on my way as planned after profusely thanking my rescuers. When I told the next unit about my misadventures, they jokingly accused me of sleeping on the job and getting my just rewards for slacking off in uniform. The situation was humorous enough that I had to join in their laughter.

Most of my air travel was done in Huey helicopters. I really came to appreciate those young hotshot, mustached Warrant Officers who jockeyed their birds across rice paddies and over mountain ridges. The airmobile innovations in Army operations were the pride of our generation of warriors. Had the chopper pilots tied scarves around their necks they would have looked as heroic and romantic in their day as did the biplane aces of WW-I when they went up against the Red Baron and his kind. When the choppers would hover close to the ground for us to climb aboard for a ride, the rotors kicked up blinding dust that clogged our sweat-stained eyes. We ducked under the swirling blades overhead, and were especially careful of the buzz saw blade on the tail that could slice open your head like a melon. When boarding aircraft, the crews told us to sit on our flak jackets for protection from ground fire coming up through the bottom of the chopper. The passengers hardly ever wore the safety seat belts that would have helped us keep our balance when the pilots sharply banked into their turns. These aerial angles made me feel like my helmet was going to roll off my head and bomb some poor farmer 2000 feet below. When I had to sit in the door gunner's seat on the side of the craft, I even thought about wearing a parachute in case I tumbled into the wild blue yonder.

The air was much cooler at the flying elevations and produced a slight chill in some seasons of the year. After living in a semi-tropical climate, I felt like wearing my field jacket when we went aloft. I had the same shivering experience when I ate in an air-conditioned cafe on a visit to Saigon. The panoramic view of the countryside from the helicopters allowed me to take some spectacular photos of the landscape. We saw jungle animals moving about in dense foliage; we skimmed over tropical beaches lined with palm trees; we watched landing craft leave white wakes in the South China Sea as they steered toward the mainland to deposit their troops; and we bobbed up and down on air drafts as we approached mountaintop positions. One sector we flew over had been bombarded with artillery shells that had made crater blasts in the terrain, leaving the land looking like the pockmarked surface of the moon. The furrowed fields of rice shoots stretched out to the horizon like a patchwork quilt made of green, brown, black and watery blue. In the highlands we saw tribal villages built on stilts sitting atop the rich red soil that blanketed the plains. I loved being up in the air, getting a heavenly view of the land below. If I am lucky, being an angel will be as exciting as flying over Vietnam.

THE CIRCUIT RIDER

Like his frontier Methodist forefathers, Chaplain Hopkins traveled extensively across the Second Corps area to see the unit personnel in forty-two scattered locations. Armed with the Bible and a camera, he recorded the scenes where he spread the good Word.

TENT MEETINGS

The 4/60 Arty was widely dispersed throughout the Second Corps Area of Vietnam. Drop-in meetings were held at every unit position. The Chaplain chatted with the men about their military engagements, heard about the status of personal relationships back in "the world," and prayed for their welfare always.

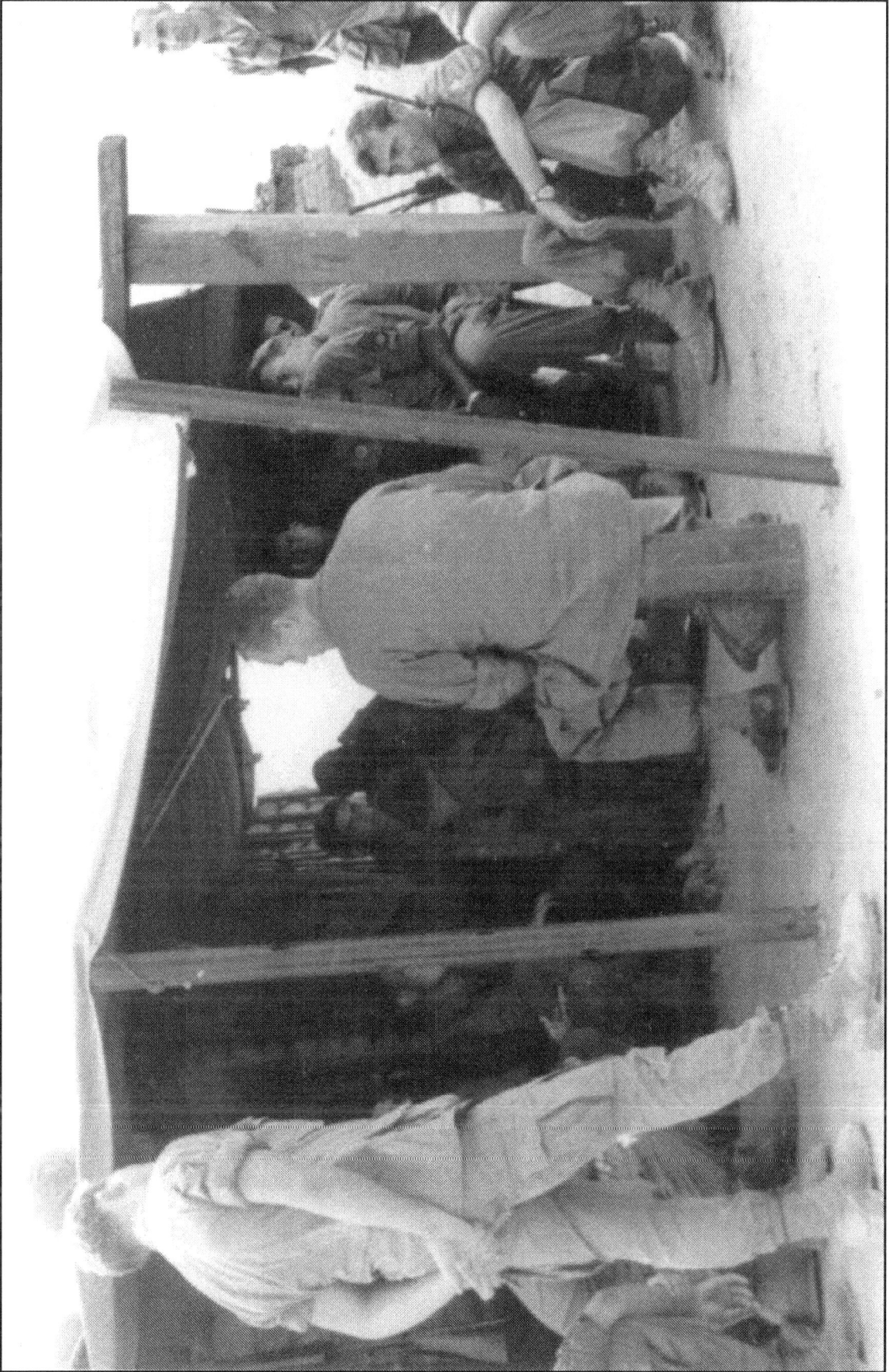

SERMON ON THE MOUNT

High above LZ Uplift in the Bong Son area of operations, one 4/60th duster crew was stationed atop a small mountain with a gorgeous view of the valley, and great fields of fire. The circuit-riding chaplain shared some gossip and the gospel with the men where ever they were stationed.

DON'T GO THERE

In case you couldn't read, a road guard halted traffic on Highway One, north of Bong Son, to prevent intrusions into enemy territory. The sign says: STOP! You are now leaving a SECURE AREA. If you can read this sign, you are too far north. TURN AROUND.

OOPS

Pity the poor traveler who had to negotiate the slippery red mud of the Pleiku central highlands during the wet monsoon season. The heavy rainfall created deep flood damage ditches alongside Highway 19, forming a jeep trap in this instance.

VUNG RO BAY

Vung Ro Bay features the azure warm waters of
the South China Sea, set against the coastal
mountains of Vietnam. Highway One zigzags
around the mountain grades overlooking the
beautiful scene below, as American troops hold
down the beaches.

SEASCAPE

The mountains slope down to the South China
Sea, with its white sandy beaches. The water
was incitingly warm, luring the troops into the
surf during the occasional secure times that
permitted such swimmingly good pleasures.

LANDSCAPE

The rice paddies have been harvested, leaving
the brown ground lie fallow. Helicopter flights
gave a heavenly perspective about that "good
earth," and the people who live on that land.

THE BOB HOPE SHOW

The troops gathered from near and far at the Phu Cat Air Base for the USO Bob Hope Christmas show. We laughed at his jokes, as he helped us over come our holiday homesickness.

CLOSE CALLS

My excursions from the battalion headquarters to our widely deployed units involved a lot of bold, unescorted, long distance driving in many directions. The 4/60 Artillery had provided me with a jeep and driver, for which I was grateful. The jeep had no radio in it, so we were generally on our own when commuting from unit to unit. From the beginning, I had to make protective arrangements for the driver and me. Only SP4 Bishop had been issued a weapon, since Chaplains are non-combatants. If we came under fire while traveling, I instructed Bishop to keep driving, assuring him that I would suppress our attackers with his M-16. As you can tell, I am not a pacifist; and neither was I foolish enough to stop moving through a kill zone so my jeep driver could become a "John Rambo" rifleman. Besides, I lettered four years on the Trinity University ROTC rifle team, and could handle firearms with the best of them when absolutely necessary. That eventuality never came, to the relief of my trusty assistant.

Most Chaplains say, when asked, they will counter fire only over the heads of the enemy if provoked into self-defense. May God forgive me, but I think I would have been inclined to aim at the offending targets to protect the lives around me. Having confessed my sinful inclinations; may I say that in the year before we landed in country, I had strongly disapproved of a newspaper picture of a "pistol-packing padre" who had been photographed openly bearing arms in Vietnam. His actions were immature, contrary to the Geneva Convention, and demonstrated basic ignorance about the limited effectiveness of an officer's sidearm in combat. The .45 pistol is a close-quarters, last resort weapon that is inaccurate beyond fifty yards. Chaplains are symbols of peace, and should play that role even at the cost of their own life, though not at the expense of other lives. Warfare never does give any of us easy moral choices.

In many respects, I led a charmed life when it came to enemy threats in Vietnam. My guardian angel was working overtime. On the other hand, I fatalistically realized that if "Charlie" wanted to kill me when we were on his back roads and dusty trails, then I was his to be taken, whenever he got good and ready. You really do have to put your life in the hands of God, and be prepared to meet your Maker, suddenly, when you are a soldier. But there were some things that we did that helped extend out stay among the living. When driving up to the Bong Son area of operations, I would check in with the battery HQ; then make trips from the main landing zone (LZ) out to the remote locations. Sometimes I would spend the night at the HQ, and other times I slept out with the detachments. On one trip we spent the night with Lieutenant James P. Miller and his men, who were camped many miles down a gravel road from Highway One. He told me as a safety precaution to sleep late the next day and let some other vehicles go back to the HQ before we departed. Sure enough, when we left at mid-morning, we came upon a five-ton truck that had hit a land mine along the road we were traveling. No one was injured because the truck was heavy enough to absorb some of the shock. Our jeep would have been blown to bits if we had run over such an explosive device.

There were several other precarious trips, when we rode over supposedly safe roads only to learn that vehicles following behind us had hit mines where our light little jeep had just driven. I guess they must have zigged when they should have zagged in the ruts of life. Our tracked vehicles occasionally had their treads blown off by mines, especially when on convoy escort duty. One crew begged me to bless their equipment to protect them from having another explosion blow up underneath them while out on search and destroy missions. Although there is no rubric or ritual for minesweeping in the prayer book, I did my best to invoke good health and safety for these frightened men. As previously mentioned, sometimes the bullets have our name on them and sometimes they are addressed to "whom it may concern."

Speaking of bullets, the only ones I ever heard whiz over my head were fired into our battalion HQ's encampment, which was the last place where I expected to duck for cover. A couple of months after our arrival, the battalion command post was moved from Phu Cat back down close to Qui Nhon in a very comfortable place known as Camp Townes, located in a valley near the Korean White Horse Division HQ. We occupied wooden barracks with tin roofs, living comfortably in a stateside like cantonment area. The cots had mosquito nets over then; the clothes closets had light bulbs in them to ward off mildew; and the mess hall served hot meals three times a day. One afternoon when I was strolling between buildings on the way to counsel a soldier who had received a "Dear John" letter, a single round sailed angrily past me, loudly banging into a tin roof like a hurling rock. The actual rifle shot had not been heard, so it took a few minutes to realize what had happened. Nervous, but curious, troops came out of their office buildings to find out what the suspicious noise was all about. No one panicked, and no alert was sounded. Our composed leaders dismissed the incident as a stray bullet that had come into the compound, saying to go back to doing whatever we were doing before the round struck the building. Easier said than done, when you're wondering if a target had been painted on the back of your helmet.

The next enemy rounds I heard and saw came at us fast and furious during the Tet Offensive of 1968, in the last week of January. By this time I was a true "short timer" due to go home on 7 February, and was operating out of the HQ compound. The VC set up an ambush across the road from our encampment, firing at convoys passing by our position. Machine gun rounds riddled our post, with bullets kicking up dust behind me as I dove for cover behind some rocks near my hilltop Chapel in the center of the compound. Two of our troops were hit, so I rushed back to Doc Anhalt's aid station to assist the wounded. One man had been shot in the face, breaking his jawbone. He was bleeding profusely from severed arteries in his mouth. The Doc asked for someone to help him by placing a hand inside the patient's mouth to clamp down on the bleeding. No one came forward to assist, so I modestly volunteered. My job was to stay alongside the trooper with my hand in his mouth, then accompany the stretcher-bearers as they carried the gunshot soldier over to the medivac helicopter. I boarded the helicopter with the patient, still clamping my hand in his jaw as the flight crew flew him to the nearest hospital in Qui Nhon. The poor fellow was conscious; I talked to him knowing that he could only answer me with his eyes. He did not moan or wince during our ride together, hopefully because the Doc has given him something to dull the pain. The chopper waffled down on the helipad at the emergency care center. The hospital doctors and nurses rushed to the patient's side, taking over his medical care in their expert manner. The next day I went back to see the wounded soldier in the recovery ward to celebrate his surviving his combat injuries. His face was so grossly swollen that I hardly recognized him. He didn't care how he looked because he was so glad to still be alive. To which I said "Amen."

The medivac chopper flew me back to the unit after we unloaded our patient. By now it was getting dark, time to hear everybody's personal version of what had happened earlier that day. The men reported that Army helicopters firing aerial rocket artillery into the enemy positions had destroyed the VC ambush. Camp Townes was safe and there had been no further casualties. Before I could hear the rest of their stories, I had to go to the aid station to assure the doctor that his patient had been delivered safely, as ordered. Before thanking me for helping his patient, Doc asked me to show him my hands to see if I had nicks or scratches anywhere. I demurred and told him that I was fine, thinking that maybe he was setting me up for a prank about being eligible for the Purple Heart. We had often kidded each other about how the Doc could make a hero out of anyone with the stroke of his pen. He kept a straight face, as I tried to laugh off his concern for my nonexistent injuries. A small crowd roared with laughter when Doc Anhalt announced that I would have to take a precautionary shot of penicillin because the man who had been evacuated had once been syphilitic. A retired warrant officer buddy of mine, Howard Funkhouser, has referred to this incident as the case of "the chaplain and the social disease." Regrettably, my Army medical records do show an entry for just that purpose. Everyone who has heard my version of the story chide me about truthfulness when telling this story, and point out that chaplains can go to hell just as much for lying as for fornication. If I hadn't been so flushed from embarrassment, I would have enjoyed the humor of the situation too. I have often wondered if that is why no one else volunteered to help the wounded man that day. Fools rush in where angels fear to tread.

To set the record straight, I did get admitted to an Army hospital during my tour in Vietnam because of an infection that had to be treated with antibiotics. In the summer of 1967, my ears became completely swollen shut from a jungle disease, with a concomitant high fever of 102 degrees. That time, Doctor Anhalt came to my rescue and insisted that I be transferred to the Medical Evacuation Hospital in Qui Nhon. By the time I arrived there, I was practically deaf. During the intake health assessment, I explained to the nurses that I had a hearing problem. They kindly noted that I was shouting at them during the interview since I could not tell how loud I was talking. The medical staff inserted treated gauze strips into my sore ear canals, supplemented with frequent injections of potent serums to combat my rampant infection. One week later I was fit for duty, though suffering afterwards a chronic case of "otitis media" (sore, runny ears) for twenty years. Vietnam gave me something to remember the time served there.

In Vietnam you often treaded dangerously without knowing it. On one occasion we had driven across Highway 19 through An Khe to visit our units assigned to the Fourth Infantry Division based in Pleiku in the central highlands. The weather was soaked from the seasonal monsoon rains, turning the red dirt roads into slippery muddy quagmires that bogged down our vehicles at times. We left the dry indoor confines of the battery's HQ compound to visit soggy remote firebases in the boonies. Usually it would be a daytime round trip to each location, meaning we could return to the luxuries of evening TV and a hot meal back in Pleiku by nightfall. But this time the Military Police closed the roads behind us after we reached our first destination, forcing us to spend the night in bunkers after conducting religious services and visiting with the men. Our change of plans was radioed back to the battery HQ, so they could account for our absence. I enjoyed the layover, accepting that travel delays were inevitable in this curious military exercise. Eating C-rations on a damp sandbag was fine with me. The next morning the muddy road was open for our return to Pleiku. To our shocked surprise, when we arrived at the HQ, there were craters dotting the grounds. The barracks where we would have been staying were riddled from shrapnel shards. The battery HQ's had suffered a mortar attack while we were stranded away from them. Being a good sport about the deprivations of being a field trooper had been rewarded that night.

On another precarious foray out of Pleiku, I was flown by helicopter to a position in the southerly direction of Ban Me Thout. There, troops of our unit were in an extremely hostile area. The duster crews excitedly showed me the fresh bullet holes in their vehicular windshields. After they calmed down, I held services, exchanged messages from and to people we knew, and counseled the anxious concerns of several troopers. The nervous chopper pilot soon said our time was up, quickly flying us away from the besieged unit only hours before the elements of the North Vietnamese Army and VC assaulted them again. Our duster crews held their ground, repulsed the enemy, and escaped injury or loss of life during that battle. Afterwards, I wistfully wondered if I could have been more helpful if I had stayed longer, or if the men would be safe during their next engagements.

By then I was off in another direction visiting troops who were wondering if their long and boring vigils would be interrupted by the deadly encounters which made combat a tedious guessing game. In November 1967, these troops were severely tested in the furious battles at Dak To near Laos, one of the largest main force engagements that ever occurred in the northern central highlands. The duster crews contributed to the American superior firepower that gave us a decisive victory on that battlefield. It's funny how you can win all the battles and forfeit a war, but you don't have time to think about those things when you are in the middle of such operations.

Most of the troops believed that chaplains were guardian angels who protected them from all harm. So much so, that they liked traveling with the "Holy Joes" when they could. As a Chaplain, I never thought of being exceptionally deserving of God's loving care and protection more than other believers. Certainly, I was very thankful for His deliverances when they had come, recognizing I did seem to get a generous share of His oversight when I was out and about. By the time I was ready to go home, He was making me totally aware that more than just good luck was accounting for my safety, particularly on one of my last exposures to hostilities. After the Tet Offensive in January 1968 was seemingly over, my chaplain's assistant drove us from Camp Townes into nearby Qui Nhon on religious business. Approaching the war torn city, we had to choose which of two turnoffs to reach the downtown area. The right side road of the juncture was the usual route to our destination, but my thoughtful driver decided to use the left side turn off to give me one last look at that part of the city.

Riding merrily along this alternate highway into Qui Nhon, I happily commented about what good travel time we were making by avoiding the usual heavy convoy traffic that often slowed us down on our regular road into town. The brisk windy day was clear and sunny, contributing to my good mood. I was going home in a few days and felt like celebrating, feeling in harmony with nature and the world. We began passing some Vietnamese Army soldiers who were patrolling the streets, giving us a false sense of security. Although nothing had happened to us, when we got to our destination, local authorities told us that there had just been some sniper attacks in the area we had just traveled - which is why the Vietnamese troops were out and about searching the city neighborhoods for the attackers. Neither the Vietnamese Army, nor the American Military Police, had posted any danger warnings on the highway we had used. The embattled road was supposed to be closed to all traffic because of the shootings. We prudently drove back to our base camp on the other route, with the realization that you are never out of danger from combat until you completely leave a war zone. The Good Lord must have needed my services still longer, since He helped me on one more occasion to escape the fowler's snare.

LAND MINE

No one was hurt (just shaken up) when the five-ton truck ran over a land mine that had been planted in a lonely village road during the night. As the chaplain, I offered thanks for these men's safe deliverance from harm, gathering the troops around the blast crater where the right front wheel of their truck had been exploded.

BLOWOUT

Platoon leader Lieutenant James Miller warned and advised Chaplain Hopkins to let a truck precede his jeep down this country road in case there were land mines. The heavier truck withstood the violent blast, losing only a front wheel. A jeep would have been destroyed by such a blast.

TET PATROL

The South Vietnamese Regular Army patrolled
the streets of all cities during the Tet Offensive,
repelling the snipers and sappers who disrupted
the security of their territory during one violent
week in January, 1968.

RAVAGES OF WAR

The Tet Offensive devastated the buildings in
many Vietnamese cities. These shops and
homes in Qui Nhon were destroyed in the brief
but intense fighting that took place in the urban
areas during January 1968.

CASUALTIES

The unit ambulance picked up a 4/60 Artillery
unit casualty during the Tet Offensive, taking
him to the Aid Station for medical evacuation to
Qui Nhon hospital. The trooper survived his
wounds, thanks to the rapid response of the
heroic medical corpsmen who were the soldier's
best friend in combat.

PASTORAL ACTIVITIES

The clergy's customary pastoral activities are to marry, bury and preach; or as one rhyming Simon once said, "we hatch, match, and dispatch." These are routine duties for a chaplain, but combat is never routine. Being in Vietnam altered the circumstances and setting for carrying out my mission considerably. For instance, when you are in a war zone subject to mortar or rocket attacks, you conduct brief devotionals near bunkers and foxholes where the troops can take cover if someone yells "incoming." Chaplains can't lollygag around very long when their services can be cut short momentarily. None of my services ever got interrupted by hostile fire I am happy to report; but I didn't tarry around either to see how long I could go before something sinister stopped me, like one of "Charlie's" Soviet built 122mm rockets.

Celebrations of religious and civic holidays were changed by the foreign context of our rituals and ceremonies. There was no time off in wartime to observe special events like Thanksgiving, Christmas, New Year's, Easter, or the Fourth of July. The tepid temperatures and tropical foliage made re-enacting American wintertime festivals seem irrelevant. If you have ever paid attention to the lyrics of Irving Berlin's song "I'm Dreaming of a White Christmas," then you recall that the subject of the tune is a nostalgic remembrance of snowy family gatherings by someone who is stuck in warm Southern California. There were no Christmas songs about being stuck in Viet Nam. The main marker for this sacred occasion was only the special military menu of turkey and dressing, with all of the trimmings of a home cooked meal.

Sweating cooks worked hard to serve the troops a tasty reminder that December 25th was a "holy day." My role was to say "Grace" at as many troop locations as I could possibly reach at their meal times. Every unit wanted the chaplain to join in their festivities literally, meaning I had to eat lunch over and over until I actually began to get nauseated with its concomitant relief. Refusing this form of communion with homesick men would have been sacrilegious, so my momentary gastronomical discomfort was inconsequential.

Interestingly enough, Vietnam provided me with a different observance of the baptismal sacrament too. One of the young troopers in my unit contracted a fervent case of religion while in country, telling me that he wanted to change his way of living and become a baptized Christian. This became a special occasion in several ways. His buddies and I were glad to see him make a change for the better in his life. He admittedly had strayed from the paths of righteousness on recent occasions, and conscientiously wanted to improve his behavior by making a profession of faith. Rather than make his sacramental rite a sober and somber ritual, the chapel fellowship decided to throw him a party, celebrating that someone we knew was becoming our spiritual brother. The chapel group decided to enjoy the occasion by throwing an ol' time countryside picnic at the site of this outdoor baptism. We brought some soft drinks and snacks out to a rice patty and flowing stream where the changed young man was to be initiated. He and I waded out into the water wearing jungle fatigues, and posed for pictures by the chapel flagstaff that was planted in the water. He took his vows, and I then performed the only full body immersion of my ministerial career as a Methodist minister. He came up out of the water to the cheers of kindred souls; and the party was on. Since then, I've always wished that civilian services would be equally as joyful and playful as the day that soldier became part of the fellowship of the church.

Anther rite under extra-ordinary conditions was a long distance wedding I performed while serving God and my country in Vietnam. An East Texas fellow came to me for counseling, after finding out that his girl friend was pregnant with their baby. The concerned young man wanted to know how to obtain medical care and benefits for her while he was on duty in Vietnam. I asked him what were his intentions regarding this woman. He tearfully said that he had planned on marrying her, but had been drafted, then shipped overseas before he could return home to have a proper wedding. This good intentioned man was totally surprised when I explained to him that the law allowed proxy marriages. The relieved trooper readily agreed to such a ceremony. We went to the nearby Phu Cat Air Base, contacting the legal services officer. The attorney helped set up a live broadcast over the worldwide radio and phone system between the girlfriend in Texas and the soldier, with me serving as the go-between. They repeated the vows I read for them, and the happy couple gratefully celebrated their legal union, though half-a-world apart. Weddings are usually a very gleeful occasion; their nuptials was one of the happiest I have ever had the pleasure of witnessing.

Some time later there was another young lad in the unit who came to me regarding his wedding. He wanted to know about his martial status after having courted a woman he met while on R&R in Japan. According to him, she was a nice girl; not someone he had picked up in a bar. He referred to her as his wife, and told about the lovely week of honeymooning they had spent together after participating in some kind of Shinto ceremony, something he hadn't understood since the vows were not in English. Frankly, I didn't know for sure what he had done and consulted with the personnel officer about the matter. While we were figuring out the situation, his ardor began to wane in only a few weeks after he returned from Japan. Finally, we told the soldier that in the eyes of Buddha he might be married, but the U.S. Army had no official records to substantiate his getting extra pay for a wife. Without a civil record of the marriage, militarily the man was considered to be still single. He seemed happy about this determination, and was advised that to prevent future complications, he ought to avoid foreign travel in Japan henceforth.

One duty often relegated to Chaplains is death notifications. When the Red Cross sent notice to the unit that someone had lost a loved one stateside, or that someone was critically ill, the chaplain was asked to deliver the message and console the grieving party. The art of giving out bad news improves with practice. I only wish I hadn't learned to become so good at it. The unexpected arrival of a chaplain in a work area could make troops nervous for fear "the death angel" was about to visit them. Hence, I would always publicly announce my purpose for visiting troops to relieve apprehensions about my being there. One day I needed to borrow a large metal pan for a chapel function, and went to visit a mess hall of a neighboring unit in our compound. I asked the dining room orderly if I could see the mess sergeant to borrow the pan. Even after instructing the enlisted man to assure the sergeant about my purposes, he strode back to get the sergeant yelling, "Sarge, come out front. The chaplain wants to see you." The poor man was trembling when he greeted me, and meekly asked if I wanted to see him about something. I set the record straight quickly. The sergeant collapsed in a chair, whereupon he lit up a cigarette to calm his nerves and get over his scare. He offered to give me anything I wanted out of his kitchen, as long as I didn't have any bad news to give him that day.

The ultimate bad news was about casualties in combat. Young deaths, violent deaths, are always the sorry consequences of warfare. When men and women are killing each other, understanding the meaning of life becomes paramount. In those battle-scarred moments, some participants get religion, while others lose their faith because of the horrors of war. During my year with the 4/60 Artillery, our unit suffered about forty-five wounded in actions (WIA's), and between five and ten were killed in action (KIA). When men died, I went to the section where they had served and held a memorial service for the survivors. My message to them was always the same:

we can bear the loss of life only if we truly believe that death is a prelude to a better world where peace reigns and love is supreme. The hard part was helping the unit commander compose the death notification letter for the next of kin. We would always emphasize the esteem the unit had for their fallen comrade, including the services and tributes held on the battlefield in his honor; assure the family that everything possible had been done medically to save his life; and lastly express our sincere deep sorrow and sympathies for their inestimable loss.

When I returned to the states at Ft. Hood, Texas, I would be on the receiving end of these family notifications and have to conduct the burial services for the returning service member. The bugler would play taps, a rifle squad would fire a twenty-one-gun salute, the casket would be lowered into the gravesite, and we would reverently present the folded American flag to the closest kinfolk. These sad rituals helped us express our grief so we could resume living.

The losses and destruction of warfare require a concerted effort to rebuild lives and the accoutrements of living. As if to offset the damages we were inflicting on Vietnam, our unit volunteered to support local civic action projects. There were ample opportunities to repair buildings, build roads, provide medical care, and donate food and clothing to deserving locals. Our headquarters was based in the Tuy Phouc district of the Binh Dinh province on the coastal side of the country. We worked through the senior American MAC-V advisor (Material Assistance Command-Vietnam) who secured projects for us from the Vietnamese military district chief (the Dai Wei). The official justification for our activities was to win over the hearts and minds of the people. The men of the chapel cared more about helping people in need than politics.

The Army had not appropriated goods for civic action projects in our unit supply system, so we had to solicit donations. Some items could be found by requisitioning excess items from the supply section that were no longer needed tactically. By chance, there were dozens of tropical sun helmets that the Army elected not to use. The Vietnamese loved to wear these hats, so we grabbed them. We found an aid agency that had surplus gallon size cans of cooking oil that was a staple for villagers, and even learned to conserve our bars of Army issued soap for village laundry donations. The advisors tactfully warned us to take the wrappers off the soap bars, so the recipients would use them for washing rather than try to sell them on the black market. The district chief informed us that his people would appreciate receiving donations of black silk material to make their clothes. The fabrics had to be bought from village shops with Vietnamese currency. I had to collect offerings from the men in the barracks to buy the cloth. Many men had exchanged military pay currency for Vietnamese piasters (the exchange rate was 118 piasters for one dollar), but rarely used them for purchases on the local economy. The men were generous with their foreign money donations since they had little appreciation of the money's value, and were easily persuaded to spend them on a good cause like chapel civic action programs. The men sincerely relished practicing charity and looked forward to presenting the goods on projects.

The Tuy Phouc district had been cited for being one of the most pacified areas in Vietnam. The project area was only ten miles from our HQ base camp, permitting convenient frequent liaison trips to the proposed civic action sites. Maybe the area was a bit too peaceful. We became complacent about our safety on one of these trips into the district. Not only were we wearing soft fatigue caps instead of protective helmets, my driver forgot to bring his rifle. Realizing we were unarmed, we nervously sped back to our unit past acres of rice patties full of black pajama laborers, hoping that the Viet Cong and the first sergeant did not find out about this security violation.

When we were surveying possible civic action projects in the district, our truckload of chapel volunteers visited a Catholic orphanage. The Vietnamese nuns greeted us without a translator; trying earnestly to communicate their specific immediate needs for assistance. We walked around the grounds and were steered toward one of their buildings. The animated nuns began saying to us, "boom boom, boom boom!" My red- faced troops were aghast, because they were frequently propositioned by prostitutes who asked them to come "boom boom" with them. They stifled their reactions until they finally recognized that the nuns were dramatizing how explosions had blown the roof off a dormitory, and they wanted the Army to repair it for them. In appreciation for our visit and prospective help, the kind-hearted nuns offered us the best hospitality they had left at their disposal by serving us indigenous refreshments. This was accomplished by a couple of sure-footed orphans scampering up some campus palm trees and cutting off fresh green husked coconuts that would be used in serving us drinks. With sharp machetes they skillfully lopped off the top end of the fruit and poured out the clear, sweet coconut juice for our enjoyment. They owned us after that.

One of these civic action projects became news worthy, gaining some positive publicity for the 4/60 Artillery in the First Field Forces military magazine. The Tuy Phouc district chief asked us to sponsor the local men and their families of the Regional Self-Defense Forces in the villages of Kim Dong and Loc Ha. These were civilian militia who guarded their own homes, while tending their fields and cattle. They had the best defense record of any similar level military unit in South Vietnam. The South Vietnamese government had only given them ammunition for their mostly antiquated guns, and nothing else. Our unit made presentations of goods at formal ceremonies. At the conclusion, a squad of Americans would extend their hands to their Vietnamese counterparts, thanking them for their splendid service by giving them some highly appreciated sundry supplies. When we mounted back onto the trucks for the return to our base camp, village children surrounded their vehicles asking for more goodies. The troops had spoiled the kids by tossing candy to them too many times when their convoys cruised down the country roads. In order to disperse the rowdy crowd of beggars, the soldiers threw a bucket of sweets on the far side of the path we were traveling. While the little ones scooped up the candy bars, the troops shifted into gear and got under way without endangering the pedestrians.

These support projects were so appreciated by the self-defense units that the Viet Cong tried to stop these civic action activities, even blowing up a building in one village that had received our assistance. This cruel destructive act was intended to warn the people not to accept our foreign aid thereafter. The enemy will surely let you know when they don't like what you are doing in their backyard. This resistance confirmed that we were doing something right, and strengthened our resolve to go back with more assistance to the villagers while we were in their impoverished, wanton country.

RICE PADDY BAPTISM

One of the troopers requested that he be baptized by full immersion. Where else better could you go than to the water pools by the nearby rice paddies? The chapel flag was planted, the vows recited, and a celebratory party was held after this confession of faith.

ORPHANAGE

The Catholic Church operated an orphanage in
our sector. The troops fell in love with the
Vietnamese children, donating money and
goods to the nuns who ran the center.

VIETNAMESE KIDS

The Vietnamese people are small in stature.
Their children often seem like exquisite, lovable
little dolls. The kids watched the Americans
carefully, in hopes of getting some edible
handouts that were called "chop chop" in
pigeon English.

CIVIC ACTION

The HHB 4/60 Artillery and E/41 Artillery donated cooking oil, powdered milk, salt, candy, toothpaste, other foodstuffs, and cloth to Vietnamese soldiers and their families in the Tuy Phouc sub-sector of Binh Dinh province near Camp Townes. The assistance program was coordinated through the MAC-V advisor and the local district chief (Dai Wei).

HELPING HANDS PROGRAM

In the summer of 1967, the men of the 4/60 Artillery collected material supplies for donations to a Vietnamese Regional Self-Defense Force from the villages of Kim Dong and Loc Ha in the Tuy Phouc District of the Binh Dinh Province. These volunteer self-defense forces had the best record of any indigenous military units in Vietnam; even though the only support they were given by their government was ammunition for their often-outdated weapons.

MORE, PLEASE

The troops were fond of distributing food and candy to the local citizens during official and unofficial civic action programs in the villages. Sometimes the enthusiastic people would crowd around the soldiers, seeking more of the goodies being offered.

WARNING

The Viet Cong blew up a community-meeting hall to protest the dusters unit having provided civic action supplies to the village defense force. The warning did not deter our allies from accepting American aid, making us even more determined to contribute to their welfare and security.

MEDCAP

Doctor James Anhalt provided treatment services to villagers in a rural dispensary as part of the unit's Medical Civic Action Projects (MEDCAP).

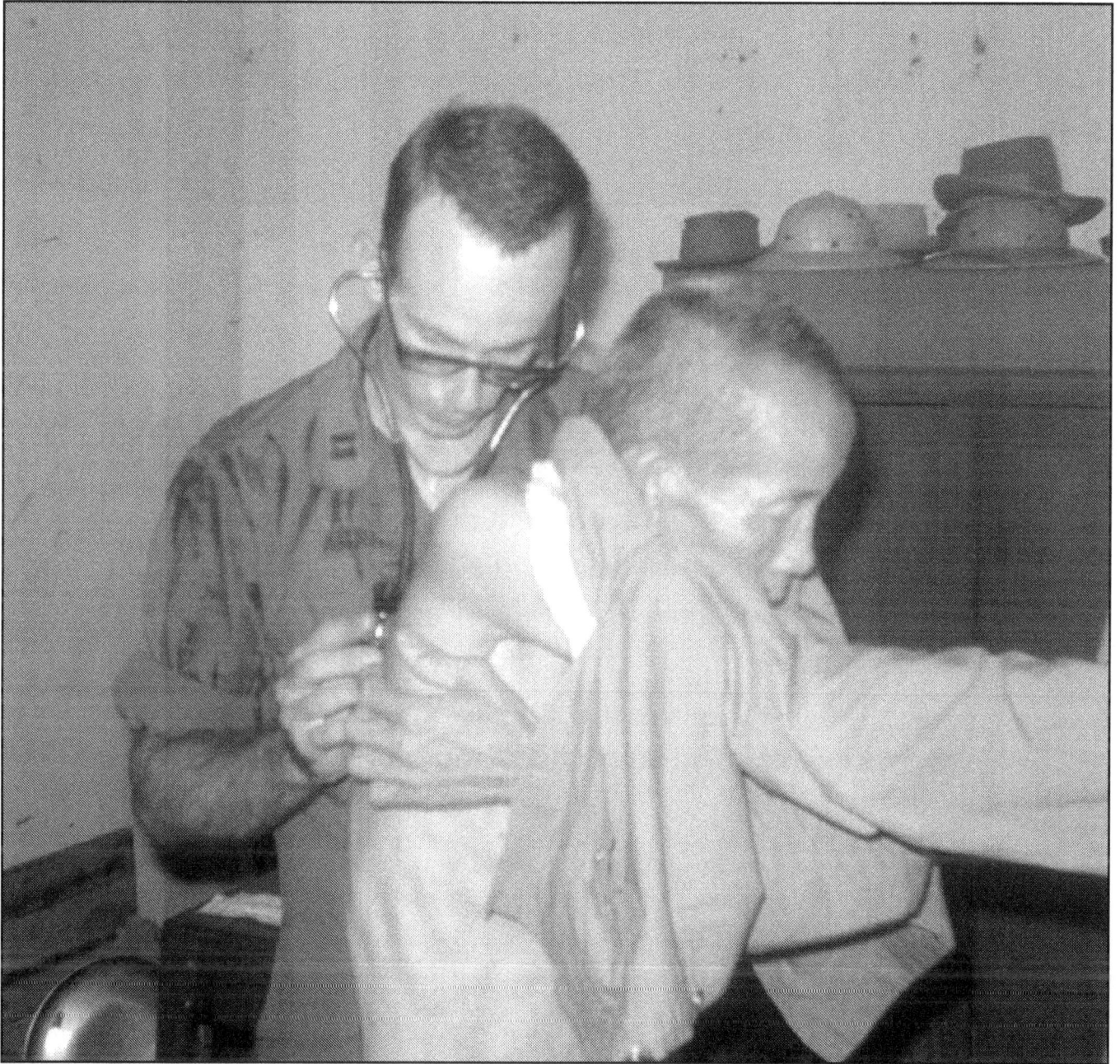

GO BOI BRIDGE

The village of Go Boi had only a peasant made footbridge to cross their river to get to the larger town of Tuy Phouc. With U.S. engineering assistance and advice, a highway bridge was built across the river. Eventually trucks were able to use the new bridge for commerce, and allied military vehicles could cross quickly when needed for protection of the Go Boi hamlet.

THE NEW BRIDGE

The Army Corp of Engineers built the new Go Boi Bridge for the benefit of local commerce and transportation. The U.S. improved the Vietnamese infrastructure for tactical and humanitarian reasons.

REFUGEE CENTER

The Caritas Catholic Charity Society of the Qui
Nhon Diocese operated a refugee center for
victims of the communist warfare. The 4/60
Artillery unit cooperated with all such local
relief programs.

TIN LANH (PROTESTANT) CHURCH

Our unit met some American Protestant missionaries who ministered to the needs of the Vietnamese through the Tin Lanh Church. The pastor gave us valuable advice about cultural customs when providing civic action programs.

MORALS AND MORALE

Humor in uniform is clever, irreverent, and ubiquitously present in the Army. Some things are repeatable and many are not. As Sergeant Major George Holloway (bless his departed soul) once told me, for most career soldiers, English is a second language; cussing is their basic means of communication. The men would develop and collect aphorisms that they used at every opportunity. Good one-liners were a status symbol. If a man woke up with a hangover, he might say that he felt like he had been French kissed by a mountain lion. One fellow, who was infatuated with the movie star Angie Dickerson, said he would make love to her in the middle of Yankee Stadium and give us an hour to draw a crowd. One flight crew painted a picture of Smokey the Bear on an aircraft used for dusting the jungle with defoliants like Agent Orange. Their slogan was, "Remember, only you can prevent forests." The men would apologize for each other (if not for themselves) when they became too profane in my presence. I assured them that I considered their trash talk to be a guarantee that I would always have a job in the Army.

The 4/60 Artillery was deployed during the height of the armed forces build up for the war. Troop discipline was still good at that time across the country. Drug abuse had not become the significant problem that developed later on in the war when America began to withdraw its ground troops from Vietnam in 1969. There were plenty of opportunities to buy drugs such as marijuana if you wanted them. The Vietnamese national government actually allowed the peasants to grow crops of pot. We used to drive by a field of "grass" where I was based, but alcohol was still the preferred means of leaving reality when the troops were off-duty, or on stand-by alert notice only. Beer and hard liquor were plentiful, and cheaply available as Class VI supplies. Booze was an integral part of military social life. My drink of choice was Coke, although I am not a blue nose or a teetotaler. We bought sodas by the caseloads at ten cents a can, drinking them to excess. My indulgences only produced frequent runs to the latrine. When the troops splurged too much, they could get rowdy. One night some men at our HQ base camp were watching an outdoor movie when the celluloid film in the projector broke. In their impatient disgust, the audience learned that the movie ending had been completely lost. They nearly rioted. To this day, I still do not know whatever happened to Peter O'Toole starring in the story of "Lord Jim." And I always worried about what would have happened if an "after hours" attack had commenced in the so-called rear areas when these men were disinhibited and less coordinated.

To counterbalance this over reliance on intoxicants in the HQ base camp, some of the men liked to gather at my chapel office after supper and visit with each other. Many of them enjoyed singing songs from the Armed Forces Hymnal, begging my volunteer organist to pump out a few more familiar tunes on the official military field organ at my disposal. He literally had to push foot pedals to make the wooden box play music. Drunken troops would sometimes peek into our informal sessions to see what we were doing, urging us to sing on key. They thought we were having a party, imagining we had consumed too much Catholic communion wine, for we were carrying on like care free patrons in an Irish pub. Part of those evenings I spent with some of the officers in their makeshift club and bar. A group of the more temperate gentlemen liked to play volleyball in preference to exercising their elbows pouring drinks. The sport was invigorating and became a wholesome alternative to the chug-a-lug life style around us. These sober minded players formed an alliance and began wearing a plastic tiger tooth on their dog tags to identify us as members of FANG, the "fraternity of awfully nice guys." We might have been God fearing squares, but were hip about it.

As in every war, one chief temptation was prostitution. The Vietnamese pigeon English term for sex was "boom boom." The women would entice the troops into their roadside bamboo huts that became known as "boom boom houses". Prices were cheap, and the troops gladly spent their money on such pleasures. Sadly, about ten percent of the troops contracted venereal diseases each month in our unit. The men who went on R&R to Bangkok, Thailand, and Hong Kong had a much higher infection rate. Inevitably, one of the field grade officers (major's rank or above) thought that one way to control the health problem would be to sponsor a unit brothel. His contention was that our medics could inspect the girls, while treating them to insure that they were free of disease. I was flabbergasted and protested profusely, but was patronizingly ignored—because Chaplains were expected to condemn such things. I even encountered an American State Department employee who endorsed the project as a means of infusing money into the local economy; to which I countered that soon the Vietnamese women would rather be laying on their backs than breaking their backs in the rice fields, if we did not stop corrupting their work ethic. The medical department defeated the scheme, by objecting that inoculating the women would only produce penicillin resistant diseases, making the problems even worse. Besides that, for security reasons, the women could not be sequestered inside the unit compound to prevent them from consorting with the Korean troops who were certain to infect them with other virulent strains of V.D. Afterwards, several other units were reprimanded for having rewarded their men with unit sponsored recreational visits to whore houses. Our unit was spared this scandal.

The young troops themselves had an ambivalent attitude about their sexual promiscuity. One of the truly great myths of military society is the widespread belief about the possible fate of infected soldiers. Purportedly, there are troops with incurable venereal diseases who are quarantined indefinitely on a secretly secluded island. The troops speculated wildly about where this place might be. Some thought the V.D. colony was off the coast of Korea, but no one knew for sure where they might be banished if they kept getting on the sick rolls. The fact that none of them could go on R&R to Australia, if they had ever contracted a sexually transmitted disease, did reinforce their conviction that there really might be an island of exiles waiting for them. Fear and guilt were alive and well in Vietnam. In my opinion, the worst moral offense our occupation forces committed was the proliferation of multi-racial fatherless babies, who were left behind to become social outcasts after the war. Antibiotic medications could not cure this pathetically immoral legacy.

Several of our troops fell in love with local girls and wanted to marry them. Military regulations, and the State Department made this almost impossible because of security concerns. Obviously, if an American serviceman had dependents in the war zone, he would be subject to intimidation and extortion by the communists. The young men simply could not understand why they could not follow their hearts' desires. The plight of the locals weighed upon their minds, while they frantically sought ways to rescue their fiancés and her family. Invariably, these frustrated men sought the aid of the Chaplains office in cutting through the red tape. One man vowed to return as a civilian after his discharge to get his intended wife. He would find out later that getting permission to re-enter Vietnam would be even more difficult than getting permission to marry while in uniform. The commanders hoped I could cool the men's ardor, but rarely have I ever talked anybody out of getting married in wartime or civilian life. The government knew that their countless restrictions and delays were the only way to limit countless refugees from immigrating to America in the midst of the war. I felt sorry for the men and their Vietnamese lovers, but believed that Uncle Sam may have been doing the right thing. War is hell when Cupid's arrow strikes a soldier's heart.

If some of the men exercised poor judgment in their conduct and relationships, their sins and errors were more than offset by the personal and political betrayals they suffered on the home front. Despite our best efforts to prepare the unit's service dependents for the effects of a yearlong separation, it did not take long after our sojourn in Vietnam for the "Dear John" letters to start arriving. Or worse yet, the wife or girl friend just stopped writing altogether, leaving the distraught soldier to wonder why. One enlisted man began to lose splotches of his hair during the anxieties of a marital conflict. To disguise his perplexities he got a super short burr haircut until his hair grew back normally. I tried to console these men and help them accept their losses; wishing the whole time that the women would hold off on announcing their breakups until we got out of harm's way. One poor fellow found out that his wife had taken all of their life's savings to run off to Las Vegas with someone she had recently met. In this case, I accurately predicted that the predator would dump his wife when the money ran out. I suggested that the soldier's real problem would be deciding whether to forgive her and take her back, once she was abandoned and longed to come back to her cuckolded husband.

Most of the time, guys who were going through such a breakup were stuck with having to cry in their beer with a few sympathetic buddies, trying to keep the man from walking out into a minefield to end his troubles. The Army would give emergency leaves out of the war zone to men who had a death in their immediate families, letting them go back home for the funerals. Yet, no dispensation was allowable for the far more painful crisis of preventing a divorce caused by a "Dear John" letter. The military knew that wartime relationships are unstable, and that troops would be forever pulling out of the front lines attempting to repair bad marriages. If the troops were allowed to take such personal leaves, they might not be willing to come back, ending up going

AWOL to get more time to win back their loved ones. The party line was, that if the Army wanted you to have a wife, then they would have issued a woman to you along with your uniforms (a very crude policy, but imminently practical as military thinking goes). While explaining these limitations of leave policies, I had men angrily throw furniture in my chaplain's office to vent their rage, and then slump to the floor in tears. Who wouldn't feel compassion for such poor souls in their misery?

A more insidious morale problem were the domestic anti-war demonstrations and urban race riots that politically divided the nation we represented. The men often sarcastically swore that if we had not been bearing arms in Vietnam, then we would have been patrolling Watts in Los Angeles, or downtown Detroit, or Washington D.C. I fantasized about what the campaign ribbons and decorations would look like for participating in riot control operations.

If you were spared the agony of family conflicts and break-ups, there were the demoralizing effects of the antagonistic Jane Fonda type dissenters who campaigned for the defeat of all American forces in Southeast Asia. I realized that troops had their doubts about the worthiness of their South Vietnamese allies; but our men were certain that the communists were a vicious enemy who mutilated children and deliberately assassinated innocent civilians in the name of a better society. As I have often pointed out to protesters, they had ignorantly confused the issue by blaming the warriors for the war. Foreign policy is made in the White House and Congress, not in the Pentagon. Promoting peace, like Joan Baez and her pacifistic husband did, was commendable. Earnest debate about our national objectives was perfectly fine. But I shall never forget the distraught Air Force waiting wife I knew in Austin, Texas, who had to get an unlisted phone number to avoid tormenting calls condemning her husband who was a POW in the Hanoi Hilton. In my opinion, the commandment to love our enemies does not include such treason. Hatred has no part in a "just war" of any kind, regardless of which side you have chosen. I did not hate the Viet Cong, and the war protestors had no right to hate the United States forces and their dependents. My hardest task has been to forgive those Americans who were so unloving of those with whom I served in the military. If Senator John McCain can forgive the North Vietnamese, who brutally tortured him for many years in their captivity, then we will have to learn how to reconcile domestically too. But Senator McCain was also right when he said that the wrong side won in Viet Nam.

AO DAI
WALKING DRESS

A Vietnamese Miss is a "Co" and her lovely
walking dress is an "Ao Dai". These proper
young ladies should be treated with respect,
and were not subject to being picked up by
some lonely foreigner.

TEMPTATION

The Vietnamese government allowed their
people to grow marijuana, which was a
forbidden substance for American forces.
During the 1967-68 tour of duty, illicit drug use
was minimal in the duster unit.

RESPITES

Picture this: an unarmed man hip shooting his way around a beautiful but dangerous country, using a Kodak Instamatic camera loaded with colored slide-making film. The hand sized instrument fitted nicely into the ammunition pouch hooked to the right side of my canteen belt. I was always armed for action and alert for targets of opportunity. Whenever I saw a picturesque site, I ordered my driver to stop the jeep, and clicked off a few "rounds" to "knock off" the scene, so to speak. Although better equipment and professional training in photography was needed, I was good at pictorial construction. I know a good subject when it is presented, in or out of a camera. Film was cheap, and I shot roll after roll of my travels in Vietnam. We could get the pictures developed through the in-country PX and have them sent home. My objective was to collect and edit a slide show for program presentations about my sojourn in Vietnam. Eventually, I sorted out enough usable pictures to fill four carousel trays for my slide projector, later converting some of the slides into prints to illustrate the adventure tales in my memoirs.

Touring Vietnam by jeep or helicopter had many visual pleasures; some were even inspirational. The countryside was so vibrantly green and lovely that the colonial French referred to it as the Riviera of Southeast Asia to promote tourism. Saigon was called the "Pearl of the Orient." When asking veterans what to expect when I got to Nam, they always referred to the beauty of the countryside as an attraction for going there. My inner fear was that the country had been defoliated, burned, and leveled from the terrible warfare. Instead, I constantly found scenes of the people and their land worthy of the National Geographic Magazine. This enamoration with the all-absorbing beauty surrounding me caused a minor conflict with my wife during our visit on R&R (rest and recuperation) leave in Hawaii. She was enchanted by the spectacular vistas on the island, but big mouthed me kept comparing them to prettier places I had seen in Vietnam. Although sincerely trying to be sensitive about her excitement amidst the truly grand experiences we were sharing, I couldn't quite suppress my awesome feelings for the country we were defending.

The trip to Honolulu came early in my tour. Four months after being away from the family, I elected to take my Army allocated R&R to Fort DuRussy, Hawaii. Patsy flew from El Paso, Texas, to meet me at personal expense. Quite by chance, my former battalion commander, Colonel William Brandt, was on the same R&R flight with me. Colonel Brandt had been gloriously promoted after our arrival in Vietnam, and reassigned to a well-deserved, cushy position in Saigon. We sat together on the plane and developed a social relationship that continued at our destination. He was meeting his wife, too. Unbeknown to me, Mrs. Kay Brandt had linked up with my wife in El Paso, so they could fly together from Texas across the Pacific. By coincidence both excited couples ended up rooming at the same hotel.

The Brandts were easily twenty years older than us, a significant difference when it came to how we wanted to spend our precious time on this vacation. Patsy and I had only been married for three years, and virtually barricaded ourselves in our room for the first forty-eight hours. I should have put a "Do Not Disturb" sign on our door to avoid the Brandt's embarrassing "knock knocks" on our door. They wanted us to come out and go shopping with them, when we passionately had other things on our minds. They still think that we didn't answer their invitations to go do things together because we supposedly were out of the room at the time they came by to get us. My wife and I stayed ever so quiet behind the locked door, trying not to giggle until they went on their way. We didn't ignore them the whole time mind you, just during the critical early moments of a wildly happy reunion. Maybe I've told you a little too much about this saucy family secret. I hope the Brandts will forgive our little deception on the basis that, back then, we were young and foolish, etc. We had another unexpected visitor that week too. My widowed mother showed up in a tour group to check on her only son and baby boy; which I didn't mind, since she found us later on in the short week of our stay in paradise when we were more amenable to having company

Eventually, we did get out of the "bridal suite," touring Oahu in a rented car. Many romantic hours were spent swimming on Waikiki beach, looking for the famous breaking waves treasured by surfboarders (they were on the north side of the island). Reclining, holding hands on the hotel veranda, Patsy and I found the fruity Mai Tai drinks to be sinfully sweet and tasty. The Hawaiian Islands produced fresh juicy pineapple that came with each culinary delight, even being served as bright yellow stirring sticks in our tall glasses of chilled ice tea. All the meals were a treat after eating institutional Army chow in Nam. We ventured around the island in our rented car to observe Diamond Head Mountain protrude above the crashing sea; watch the blowhole exude geysers of foaming sea spray upon the craggy coastal cliffs; climb up a jade colored jungle trail to refresh ourselves by the streaming cascades of a pristine waterfall; marvel at the rib backed, mossy green mountain ridges; and admire the miles and miles of cultivated plantation fields filled with ripening pineapples and bananas. From the spectacular mountain heights we could see the somber Pearl Harbor memorial, the final watery resting place for so many American naval heroes of WW-II. For entertainment there was the latest James Bond movie, "You Only Live Twice." We bought and wore Hawaiian clothes to tour the Polynesian Village theme park (owned by Mormons, I might add). My lady looked fetching in her alluring muumuu dress bedecked with a white floral lei, and I liked sporting a gaudy, native design, Hibiscus flowered print shirt (the opposite of camouflage combat dress). We should have stopped the touristy thing of trying to see everything and do everything in a limited time, before we took a fateful party boat bay cruise. While learning to do the hula on the swaying deck, poor Patsy got miserably seasick, retching herself weak, as if to prove, we may have been in paradise, but it wasn't the Garden of Eden.

Returning to strife filled Vietnam from such a romantic and peaceful Hawaiian holiday was very difficult; so much so, that many men I counseled declined to going on R&R to avoid this re-entry problem. Obviously, the brief marital closeness re-opened the longing to be back with family and friends. When I unpacked my clothes back at the HQ in Camp Townes, the jocular men spotted my Hawaiian print shirt, giving it a crude nickname. They called such civilian clothes the "got some" shirts (don't make me explain the inference about my love life). Their good natured taunts broke my melancholy mood, grinding me back into the rough realities of being a holy man counseling and comforting men at war; where troops must concentrate on survival and forget about home, if they expected to see their loved ones again.

Whenever I was absent from the 4/60 Artillery HQ base camp, I arranged for someone to conduct the weekly, formal Sunday worship services in the chapel. While on R & R, one of the unit's most dedicated soldiers, SP4 Ron Sparks, kindly and competently delivered an inspiring sermon to the faithful, fatigue clad congregation. And why not? After all, in civilian life he had been a minister in the Salvation Army. Unfortunately, at the time he was inducted into the Army, he was not eligible to become a commissioned military chaplain. I am pleased to report that later in his civilian career, he did earn such an appointment as a chaplain in the U.S. Army Reserve after the Vietnam War was over. SP4 Sparks greeted me warmly upon my return from R & R, giving a full report of his activities; well, nearly a full report.

As I was making my customary visits in the troop barracks, I spied the Army issued Jewish chapel flag hanging on the wall as a decoration over someone's bunk. Quickly, I sought out my surrogate preacher to gently investigate how this sanctified flag, with the white tableau of the Ten Commandments on a navy blue background, had been filched from the chapel storage locker while I was on leave. Poor man, thinking the item was a disposable, excess commodity, Rev. Sparks had lent the flag to a curious non-Jewish soldier who wanted to display the attractive design in his living area. Once he understood the significance of this flag, Sparks rushed pell-mell back to the barracks to retrieve the precious religious symbol, explaining to his bunkmate that only a Rabbi was allowed to designate his office or quarters with the cloth insignia on loan to him. Both men apologized profusely for their unintentional sacrilege. The soldiers were quickly absolved of any imaginable offenses after examining them about whether they knew how to perform Bar Mitzvahs or Seder meals for Passover. No harm had been done as long as the supply sergeant was kept out of the situation.

Happily, the resumption of frequent forays across the Second Corps of Vietnam provided me with many interesting sidelights, helping occupy my wandering attention while counting down the time left in my tour. Chaplains had a special responsibility as special staff officers to the unit commander to be informed about the religions of our host country. Buddhism was prevalent among the Vietnamese. Our first important cross-cultural lesson was to recognize that the Buddhist symbol for enlightenment and salvation looks like the swastika. The insignia is an old and honorable design in the Far East. The Buddhist tombstones were frequently marked with what looked to us like a hated Nazis emblem. The Buddhist shrines guarded by ornate porcelain temple dogs, the red baked brick pagodas, the outdoor devotional altars, the giant sized statues of Buddha, and their multi-colored religious flags intrigued my mind and my senses. Buddhist monks of all ages, adorned in yellow robes, walked along the highways, and could occasionally be seen meditating in their simple, sparsely furnished, bamboo huts. My seminary course on the religions of the world had become a living exercise in diversity.

Troop visitations regularly took me into the rugged central highlands, where I could observe the primitive religion of the indigenous Montagnard tribes. They carved totem figures to adorn their thatched huts and central meeting hall. The ornaments looked like the wooden carvings made by early Native Americans seen in museums and movies about the wild, wild west. Many of their animistic beliefs seemed superstitious to modern minds; and regrettably, the Vietnamese looked down upon Montagnard tribes as ignorant, uncivilized savages. These tribal people are dark skinned and live in a cooler climate than the coastal areas of Vietnam. Their acclimation to the elements amazed me, wearing only loin clothes in weather where I needed a long sleeve shirt for warmth. The tribal bare-breasted women were a popular G.I. curiosity, prompting the troops to dub them the Montagnard "a' go-go's." A Chaplain's job is never done.

Traipsing around Vietnam was not complete without finding some pretense to do business in Saigon, the Paris of the Orient. Our unit was considerably up-country (300 miles or more) from the capital city that was close to the steaming Mekong Delta. The distance apart made boondoggles into the capital city more difficult and, therefore, all the more challenging for our troops to accomplish. My scheme as a prospective world traveler was to apply for an official passport that could only be issued by the U.S. Embassy, and had to be picked up in person at that agency. This passport was unexpectedly needed later in the year, when I secured an elective R&R trip to Hong Kong. After getting permission to fly on official business into the Tan Son Nhut Air Base, I stayed in a downtown Saigon hotel that had been requisitioned for the duration of the war to serve as a BOQ (Bachelor Officers Quarters). To my surprise the BOQ housed American Red Cross workers. Round-eyed women seemed out of place after being in the boondocks so long. The accommodations were exceptionally comfortable in this urban environment. I asked the residents how they could tell that we were in the midst of a great war, unless they read about it in the Stars and Stripes newspaper. Front line troops always scoff, out of envy, at the luxuries in the so-called rear areas, unless they got to enjoy the air conditioning and fancy food too.

The bureaucratic delay in processing my passport allowed for several days of free time to ride around Saigon in colorful blue and yellow Renault taxicabs to tour the wide, tamarind tree-lined boulevards and see the famous landmarks of the city (the fancy hotels, statues of native heroes, and the national congressional building). We fought the traffic on Tu Do Street with its many G.I. bars and strip clubs, all the way down to the riverfront floating restaurants. Saigon is a major inland port with large tankers and freighters anchored in the rapidly flowing river currents. After we rode by the presidential palace, I thought I saw the very attractive premier's wife, Madame Ky, at a public ceremony. She was wearing the traditional Vietnamese "ao dai" walking dress, that consisted of a long silk tunic with slits on the sides and worn over loose fitting trousers. I was mildly amused to see that cosmetic surgery had been performed on her eyelids to make her look more occidental. One afternoon I shopped in the bustling Cholon Chinese neighborhood, admiring the exquisite porcelain dishes and figurines. Later that day, I strolled through the orchid filled national botanical gardens, and fed a few exotic animals in the park's zoo. Supper was some fabulous French cuisine at the famous Continental Hotel in the central district. The menu offered Algerian wines (imports from another former French colony) to accompany the swellegant food. The issuance of my passport served to evict me from further urban self-indulgence, necessitating my return to the conflicted countryside.

In the ninth month of my tour, I was offered another R&R on a stand-by availability basis. My first choice was Bangkok, to meet an Air Force chaplain buddy, Swede Erickson, who was in Southeast Asia also. I sent Swede my intended travel dates to coordinate a rendez-vous with my old college and seminary classmate. When I reported to the busy R&R processing center in Cam

Ranh Bay, the flights to Thailand were full. The center staff gave me an alternative space available trip to Hong Kong instead, which I elected to take rather than miss out on this bonus vacation. My close friend, Captain Jim Anhalt, M.D., was in the same situation, and agreed to go along with me for company. Since both of us had passports, we agreed to tour Hong Kong, then purchase commercial airline tickets, flying as civilians from there to Bangkok. When traveling on military status, troops did not need a passport to enter a country for R&R. We kept copies of our original permissive orders for traveling to Bangkok, knowing if our Thai destination was reached, that we would be allowed to catch free military transport back to Vietnam using the worthless orders that had been issued to us. The plan worked to perfection, and I have the pictures to prove it.

Upon landing in Hong Kong, the flight crew played a joke on the passengers by announcing that all of the bars and sin palaces were temporarily closed in observance of a local religious holiday. The party-minded troops groaned at this incredibly bad news. A round eyed, blond American stewardess facetiously paused on the microphone before lifting the fictional prohibitions with an earthy laugh, thereby preventing a riot in the aisle ways. I was probably the only soldier who was not upset with this inauspicious welcome. After receiving an orientation briefing about the do's and don'ts of visiting this British Crown Colony, the robust men then literally stampeded down the exit ramp from the plane. The strangest part of the visit was hearing local Chinese speak "the King's English" with a proper British accent. Hong Kong, being a duty free port, offered many great bargains on goods and services. Although preferring to spend my time and money on sightseeing, I did commission a tailor-made, "James Lee and Company," suit for eveningwear at the many fancy dining establishments featuring floorshows and seven course meals. The suit fit fine, as long as I stayed trim and fit from the constant exercise of living in the field. Upon returning stateside, despite the usual pledges to work out vigorously, I regained the weight lost in Vietnam plus a few pounds more. The Hong Kong suit was soon stored in the back of a closet in hopes of slimming down again some day to fit into those fine clothes. This never happened, and some years later the classy duds were donated to a Goodwill Industries Clothing Sales Store.

Thanks to a series of guided tours, I rode a cable car up the steep peak on Victoria Island to view the colony's grandeur; then heard the screaming hordes living in the crowded tenants of Kowloon, where the only way for privacy was to put cotton in your eyes and ears; saw the boat people living and cooking on junks in New Aberdeen Harbor; then rambled through the Tiger Balm theme park (built by the wealthy owner of a popular rubbing ointment company); saw thousands of impoverished refugees from mainland China living on the hillsides in cardboard huts; and came within 100 yards of the militarized border guarded by the Chinese Red Army. Having seen the face of our communist adversaries, Doc and I were feeling adventuresome and elected to take a risky tour by aerofoil boat to the nearby Portuguese colony of Macao, at the muddy mouth of the Canton River. The United States, earlier in 1967, had suspended diplomatic relations with Macao, because of incursions and demonstrations by the "communistic revolutionary red guards" in that territory. As we were soon to see, those malicious red guards had painted propaganda slogans on public buildings and walls during their raids. A large red lettered sign along one street fence said "Long Live Chairman Mao."

Doc and I were warned beforehand that if we were taken captive, or got into legal difficulties on our trip, the U.S. State Department could not intervene on our behalf. Nevertheless, we used our passports to exit Hong Kong for Macao and chanced the thirty-mile day boat trip along the coastline of the People's Republic of China. The smiling, obsequious tour guide frequently assured us about our personal safety, so we would be confidant of an uneventful return that evening to British protection (Would a "Lotus Tour Company" employee lie about a thing like that just to make a buck?).

Macao is a small compact island whose main attractions were the floating casinos that attracted the wealthy citizens of Hong Kong, where gambling was illegal (Chinese love to gamble, we found out). I don't indulge in the vice, but was curious about the games of chance the Chinese played. One casino table involved betting on how divisible was a pile of buttons. The casino operator used a croupier's stick to count out the buttons from the stack by sorting them out four buttons at a time. The objective was to see if a stack of buttons was evenly divisible by four, or if there would be a remainder of one, two, or three buttons, after all of the pile had been completely counted. This button counting game proved you could bet on anything if that was your wayward desire. Serendipitously, the casino visit introduced us to Chinese classical opera that was being performed to entertain culture-loving customers. The mask-like exotic makeup and ancient costume garb were better than the strange sounding music. In the bay surrounding the isle of Macao, three Red Chinese gun ships menacingly patrolled the brackish waters, reminding the inhabitants and their touring guests who was in charge in this part of the world. After a good meal of golden fried prawn in a bay side bistro, and one last look at the façade of an old Portuguese Catholic mission, we happily and discretely slipped away from Macao without notice or fanfare. Doc Anhalt and I didn't want to stay any longer than planned, no matter how well we would have been treated as detainees.

Flying from Hong Kong to Bangkok, our commercial civilian flight plan took us across the nighttime skies of Vietnam. The excited civilian passengers peered out their windows to catch glimpses of illumination flares glowing against the clouds. Doc Anhalt and I were unimpressed by the tiresome sights below, not needing any reminders of what was waiting for us when our vacationing was over. The best part of our trip was just ahead in the most exotic place I ever visited in the Far East. If I ever revisit any of the few oriental places I have seen, send me to Bangkok—please. We hired a cab to take us to the R&R orientation center to get a hotel room and register our presence in Thailand, so we could get back to Vietnam later. The briefing officers explained to the troops that one of the most important local customs they had to respect during their visit concerned fraternization with Thai women. Under no circumstances was there to be any public display of affection, not even with the girls they had hired for companionship (the pros). I want to add that Bangkok had the highest rate of venereal disease infections among troops returning from R&R. In those days HIV had not become endemic as it tragically has become today in the land of "The King And I."

Bangkok is a tourist's paradise with its brightly colored Buddhist temple roofs and gold embossed monuments. My friend Swede met me as planned and served as my tour guide. His Air Force duties had frequently brought him into the capital city on business, and he knew just where to take me in the time available. We climbed the Temple of the Moon; sailed along the floating markets of the Chao Phraya River; saw the changing of the ceremonial robes on the precious emerald Buddha by Thai royalty; and admired the intricately ornate carvings around the numerous wat compounds (monasteries for monks). The Thai monks wore orange robes, and I caught a couple of them wearing sunglasses and smoking cigarettes. Naturally, I went to the local Thai theme park to watch elephants roll teak logs, cheer for kick boxers fighting a few rounds, cringe while a snake charmer piped a tune before a weaving cobra, and admire the graceful traditional native dancers preen and prance through their ancient ritual movements.

In the evening Swede and I supped scrumptious, spicy Thai foods. By day I shopped in the jewelry stores that are always around the corner from where you are staying. Thailand produces almost any precious stone you might want to buy, except diamonds. The customers sit at long counters and indicate what jewelry they are seeking. The smiling shopkeepers bring out trays of valuable loose stones, plentiful as creek gravel. I searched through a thousand small star sapphires, while a gentleman next to me combed through a tray of rubies. The customers pick out and match the stones they want to buy and have mounted in bracelets, broaches, and necklaces. Americans find that Thai jewelry has too much gold in it to hold mountings tightly, so they frequently buy only loose stones. The other popular purchase item was Thai raw silk ties. I bought a rainbow of colored cravats for every man in my family. Where did all of the time and money go?

The leave was over, and it was time to go back on combat duty. We caught a ride on the embassy flight back to Saigon. Once back in Vietnam, we flew on military transports northward to Qui Nhon to be picked up by our drivers, and returned to the base camp full of stories about our world travels. Providing you live to tell about it, the Army will take you many places and provide you with plenty of experiences worthy of publication. By the way, if you are interested, I have the phone number of a friendly recruiting sergeant who wants to get to know you better.

HONOLULU R & R

Like many other happy couples, these lovebirds
met in Honolulu during the R & R (rest and
recuperation) leave granted to soldiers during
their tour in Vietnam. The wives flew from the
continental USA to Hawaii at personal expense
in order to enjoy a six-day respite from the war
and family separations.

WOMAN
AT THE WELL

The villagers used a public well to supply their
homes with drinking, cooking and washing
water. This scene looks Biblical, and reminds
us of how Jesus once met a Samaritan woman at
Jacob's well, telling her that he knew that she
had more than one husband.

WATER HAULING

The Vietnamese farmers manually lift their
irrigation water into the rice paddies by swinging
a bucket on long ropes back and forth from a
stream into the fields. It takes two workers many
backbreaking hours to do this task.

WATER WHEEL

The river current powered a hand made bamboo
water wheel that lifted the stream up into a
viaduct for use by the villagers in the An Lo
valley of the Bong Son area of operations.

THRASHING RICE

After planting the rice shoots in their paddies,
harvesting them when grown, the villagers beat
the rice stalks to separate the grain from the
shafts. The climate permitted two and three
growing cycles each year. Vietnamese farmers
were always hard at work, even when battles
raged around them.

RICE HAULING

The villagers carried their thrashed rice to the
market in a time honored fashion—on their
backs and shoulders.

RICE CAKES

The village cooks made rice cakes that looked
like tortillas, with the food being dried on
bamboo racks. Sometimes passing traffic
contributed a fine film of red dust to flavor the
white disks.

BUNDLE OF
RICE CAKES

These rice cakes were being carried to the
village market; but the road was long, so the
Vietnamese porter stopped for a rest in the
shade of a palm tree that hot summer day.

VILLAGE MARKET DAY

Early each morning the villagers would buy and
sell their wares to each other, as had been their
rural custom for eons. Small freshly caught
fish, bowls of recently harvested rice, duck
eggs, live animals, kitchen goods and other
necessities were exchanged. U.S. troops were
discouraged from buying or eating this produce
for sanitary reasons.

RIVER CANAL

Vietnam is full of waterways for transportation and fishing. The boatman was passing by the village of Go Boi that had been the scene of heavy fighting earlier in the conflict.

SALT FARM

The Vietnamese produced salt by irrigating
seawater into evaporating pools. They gathered
the brine's residue into salt piles before
shipping the product into the economy.

FARM BOY

Young Vietnamese boys worked as family
herdsmen in the village fields. They guided the
large water buffalos using a small stick as
bravely as when David met Goliath.

OLD MAN WITH UMBRELLA

An old Vietnamese man walked under his umbrella in the semi-tropical sun down Highway One, as Army trucks rumbled on missions.

HORSE CART

An enterprising villager built a horse drawn
jitney cart for local transportation. The people
walked, rode bicycles, or caught rides on any
moving conveyance to get places. There were
few privately owned cars anywhere.

LAMBRETTAS

The Lambretta was the most common
motorized vehicle of the Vietnamese people.
They hauled passengers and produce, usually
heavily loaded with both.

BUDDHIST SHRINE

The Buddhists practice private devotions and set up religious altars throughout Vietnam for use by faithful believers.

CHECK POINT
CHARLIE PAGODA

This ancient Buddhist shrine (circa, 938 A. D.)
overlooked Highway One and the American
encampment at Check Point Charlie. The
Signal Corps set up antennas on this
promontory to communicate with men, much
like the pagoda was built to communicate with
one's inner-self for the attainment of Nirvana.

BUDDHIST TEMPLE

A temple dog sits upon an ornate pillar to guard the entrance of a Buddhist temple against evil spirits who might try to enter into the place of worship. The buildings have Chinese style roofs and decorations.

BUDDHA

Buddhism is one of the three great religions in Vietnam. The swastika is their symbol of enlightenment and is used to decorate idols and tombstones. This statue was built at Check Point Charlie near Qui Nhon in the Tuy Phouc sub-sector.

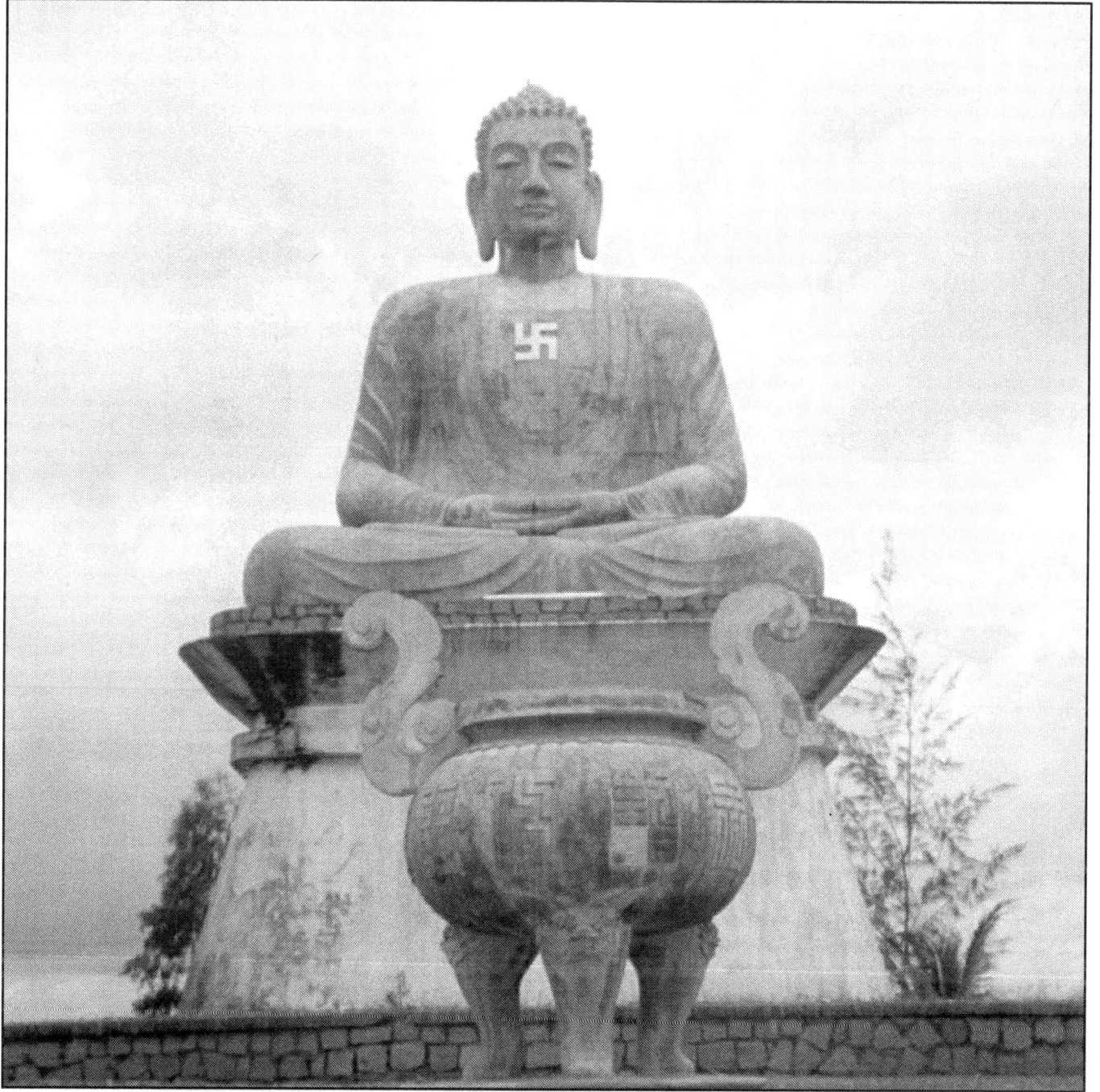

MONTAGNARD VILLAGE

The Montagnards are a primitive tribal people
who live in the Vietnamese highland areas.
They were loyal allies who used crossbows to
hunt small animals. Their bare breasted women
only wore skirts, prompting the G.I.s to call
them the "mountain girls a' go-go."

TRIBAL TOTEM

The Montagnard tribes carved totem figures as part of their religion. Their beliefs are a form of animism in which everything has a spirit, including trees, rocks, and animals. Meeting the mountain people was like a trip backwards in time.

CAREER CONFLICTS

In military principle, I might have been spared from much of my circuit riding, since the 4/60ᵗʰ Artillery personnel were supposed to have been served by the chaplains of the units where they were assigned. The Chaplains Corps espoused a goal of serving all troops within the immediate area of their unit's sector of operations. In actual practice, every commander wanted the assigned chaplain to concentrate on his particular unit. Since a chaplain's officer evaluation rating (OER) was made by his immediate commander, the area coverage of outside elements became a secondary mission at best for the chaplain of the unit to which he was attached. Hence, riding the circuit had been a necessity, to ensure the provision of religious services for our own troops. I wanted to keep up with these men even if they had been receiving adequate local coverage, which they sometimes weren't getting. The time consuming priorities of frequent troop visitation eventually created a career conflict with my third and last battalion commander.

A self-aggrandizing lieutenant colonel, who transferred into the unit from a soft rear area desk job, decreed that a newer and bigger chapel building must be constructed in the headquarters base camp, despite having just finished building a place of worship for the previous battalion commander, Major Willie Haywood. This new construction project detracted from the time that I could spend riding the circuit. My job was building lives, not erecting buildings. Still, orders are orders; so I set about trying to balance the extra demands of a dubious monument to someone's ego with the more important job of tending to the scattered flock in the fields. The chapel in question was completed before I left Viet Nam, thanks to my contacts across the Corps area where I had been visiting.

Chapel construction had a very low priority in the Army's material supply program. In order to make building improvements, much less erect a new structure, we had to scrounge up the materials needed for the chapel project. The logistical support system had not allocated any resources for the building that the new commander wanted. Still, when he looked across the valley from Camp Townes, he enviously spied a "gerry-rigged" rock cathedral in a nearby Army Aviation compound that he coveted. To make matters worse, that particular helicopter outfit occasionally few into our little camp to pick me up when they needed a "fill-in" Chaplain to conduct services in their lovely building, especially when they had suffered combat casualties.

Thanks to the good will of the troops, chapel building projects received precious donations of services and goods. Their contributions were especially needed, more than ever, for the unreasonable demands that were placed upon me. Commanders don't care how you get a job done, as long as they get what the want. Such self-serving abuse of authority was responsible for the multifarious bootleg operations instigated outside of regular supply channels to meet these so called "command requirements." Under a previous battalion commander, there had been a requirement to cover the frame of the chapel building with a tin roof, instead of using the tent canvas that had sheltered it. Even this seemingly small building improvement was a difficult assignment because the 4/60th didn't have any metal sheets for the chapel. Hearing about the chaplain's plight, one enterprising duster crew section in the Tuy Hoa area sent us word that the nearby air base was building new barrack huts. In the Air Force work area, some sheets of tin were laying on the ground, awaiting use for roofing. The duster crew invited me to come down for a visit, suggesting that I bring a trailer with my jeep, in case I found some surplus tin to haul back to my chapel site.

Now bear in mind, I urgently needed to roof the chapel, but didn't want to commit a crime by breaking the eighth commandment about stealing. The trusty old sergeants of the unit assured me that reallocating government supplies wasn't stealing as long as it stayed in the system and there was no personal gain from the transaction. I liked their rationale, and swiftly lifted a pile of tin from the air base to bring back to Camp Townes for the chapel roof. I commented to those involved that the mission of the Air force was to provide "cover" for the Army, and that the new roof would symbolize that relationship. Besides, we could pray daily for the flight crews in payment for this donation, even if they were unaware of their generosity. But God reminded me that honesty is required when procuring goods for a righteous cause. While I was nailing the Air Force tin on the Army chapel, I smashed my thumb with a hammer so hard that the battalion aid station had to cut a hole in my thumbnail to relieve the pressure and drain out the blood from this throbbing injury. I never misappropriated tin again. Then again, I didn't need any more of it to finish the roof either. Someday I will have to do some penance for this transgression.

When the order came down to build a completely new chapel, the acquisition of construction materials was even more involved than the clandestine tin snatching caper had been. The troops had to find bags of non-existent cement to pour a concrete pad for the foundation. Scarce lumber for the walls and rafters miraculously appeared for the carpentering. Invaluable tarpaper and roofing shingles, from who knows where, arrived when the framework needed "drying in." The clincher occurred when one group of men went on a mission to Saigon, and bought some colored glass windowpanes for use in designing a stained glass window for the chapel. They had taken up a voluntary collection to pay for the green and gold sheets of glass. How they transported the breakable items hundreds of miles without damaging them in any way was a minor miracle in itself. One of the dedicated sergeants of Headquarters Battery made a window frame to mount the glass. The decoration filled the wall behind the chapel altar, and was made so that the glass formed a gold cross against a green background. The morning sun showed through this adornment, brightening up the chapel during worship services and inspiring us.

Despite my original misgivings about the time and materials consumed to complete this chapel project, we took special delight in seeing this house of worship magnificently perched on the hill in the center of the compound. My commander thought the building should have been finished sooner than it was. To show his displeasure, he gave me a critical officer's evaluation report, which I had to refute through written testimonials from the officers and men whom I had served. My record was corrected once I got back to the states; but it took one full year to substantiate and vindicate this part of my performance of duty.

The conflict was a simple one in essence. I was out in the boondocks with the men more than their own commander. Once we had two men killed when their jeep rode over and detonated a mine on Highway 19 as they were delivering hot food to a crew at a checkpoint protecting a key bridge on the road. The battery headquarters in Pleiku had requested that I conduct a memorial service for their fallen comrades at the HQ, and at the site in the field where the men had died. Other than myself, no one from the battalion HQ staff came over from Camp Townes, located on the coastal side of the country, to the highlands site for the services to pay their respects to the dead. Since we had had very few fatalities in the whole unit, this was a memorable occasion for all those involved. The absences of key battalion staff were noted by the men in the field, in contrast to the religious assistance that was rendered in their time of mourning. That's why my officer's evaluation report was eventually negated, and my career subsequently continued despite the one commander's prejudicial attempt to ruin it in Vietnam.

One time a battery commander really thought that I had permanently ended my career all right, because of my unaccounted for presence in his area. SP4 Bishop and I had left from the battalion HQ heading toward the battery commander's location, but had been held up all day at a checkpoint in An Khe, until the road ahead had been cleared of a treacherous ambush. Our convoy was not released until it was nearly dark, and there were several hours of driving left to get to our destination. Upon arriving at the battery headquarters, the unit personnel expressed their worried alarm about our being so late. They had radioed back to higher HQ's, reporting us as missing, perhaps even killed or wounded in action during the violent ambush on Highway 19 where we had just traveled. The problem was compounded by the simple fact that my jeep was not equipped with a radio that would allow communications with our counterparts about our delay in travels.

Jeep radios were a status indicator, and the chaplain's section had a very low priority when it came to these type categories of rationed equipment and supplies. Radios were for the combatant soldiers, and we were just support service functionaries. I felt like those of us who were the most frequent travelers should have been given the protection radios afforded; necessities for roadrunners like myself. The unit leaders were glad to learn that we were safe and sound since bad things often happened to lightly armed travelers such as my driver and me. Loss of a chaplain would have created a monstrous morale problem for any command, because of the implications that nobody, not even a man of the cloth, was safe in a war zone. I was flattered that they cared so much about our safety, and apologized for having worried them so much by the unavoidable delay created by the ambush. The problem could have been avoided, but the battalion HQ never did install a radio on my jeep to eliminate such future incidents.

Once I arrived at the various field locations, I had opportunities to observe how the battalion headquarters interacted with its subordinate units. Even though I was on the battalion staff, battery personnel accepted me as someone acting on their own organizational level. This perspective helped me become party to their conflicts with the headquarters I represented. On one occasion, elements of Alpha Battery were protecting the perimeter of a large coastal firebase at Phan Thiet for the Seventh Cavalry. The battalion HQ radioed to them that all personnel were to be put on an emergency alert for the next 24 hours due to an expected enemy offensive. The battery was ordered to put two people in every defensive position at all times. Now this presented a problem for Alpha Battery, because they were at seventy-percent personnel strength, and obviously didn't have enough men to position two people everywhere.

When the battery reported their predicament to HQ's, they were told there would be no exceptions. The battery commander replied that even his first sergeant and the lieutenants were pulling guard duty to help man positions. There was simply no one left for assignment to all posts as mandated. Military personnel know that guard duty is customarily performed by lower ranking soldiers, and is never, repeat, NEVER, done by "top-kicks" or officers. Despite the battery's earnest attempt to comply with these ludicrous orders, the HQ's radioed back, that despite personnel shortages, the battery MUST put two people on every guard post. The battalion HQ feebly explained that this requirement was dictated by "higher ups." It was clearly an impossible situation. The battery staff muttered a number of uncomplimentary things about the Neanderthal ancestry of the "ticket-punching officers" who were issuing such "dumb orders." Being a chaplain, naturally, I said, "Amen." The hapless battery commander did the only thing possible that would resolve the problem; he radioed back to the battalion HQ's that the order had been accomplished. At first I was appalled at this insubordinate deception, and then, I realized his answer was brilliant. Under the circumstances wherein a system will not accept truth for an answer, then it deserves the answers it gets. That interaction epitomized for me the inherent unreliability of the military reporting system during the Vietnam War. I learned a valuable lesson in contextual ethics that day in Phan Thiet.

That lesson came in handy later when I returned to the "real world" from Vietnam in 1968, and was assigned to the Second Armored Division based at Fort Hood, Texas. As a brigade chaplain, I had inherited the "best-attended" Protestant chapel service on the post. Each week the Division Headquarters required that my staff report how many troops and their dependents had been at Sunday services. One day I got a phone call from a senior sergeant at the HQ inquiring if the chapel attendance figures reported were accurate. I unassumingly asked the enlisted men in my charge if they were confident of these figures, thinking that maybe there had been a fudge factor in the headcount to keep up our numbers in order to maintain our top ranking for chapel attendance. The guys understood their tasks well, assuring me that they had not inflated the report. Sunday's attendance had been normal; the reported figures were in line with the usual numbers of people present at worship services. When returning the phone call to the Division HQ's, I confidently replied that we had checked on our report and knew the attendance figure was accurate. The high command asked us to check the reports again. "Certainly," I replied, puzzled about what they thought might be discrepant. The Division HQ's suggested that we should be sure to count the ushers and the choir members in reporting totals. The message was clear: someone wanted, or needed, higher numbers for our chapel attendance, just like many combat commanders in Vietnam who demanded higher body counts in keeping track of the won/lost record of the war.

If truth is the first casualty in combat, then our duster unit helped put some nails in honesty's coffin. One hot, humid evening at dusk in the HQ base camp, a new executive officer with some fellow officers were observing some dusters fire some H&I (harassment and interdiction) rounds into the dark, hostile mountains surrounding our position. The 40 mm rounds were slamming into the ridgeline in order to discourage any Viet Cong or NVA soldiers from trying to set up mortar or sniper positions to fire into our compound. Suddenly, the major exclaimed that some rounds had erroneously gone over the ridge. Other, more seasoned officers immediately informed him that nothing like that had happened. The major incredulously asked them if they were blind, or had simply missed seeing the rounds fly over their target. Trying to be helpful, the operations section officer blithely explained to the new executive officer that none of them wanted to be witnesses about rounds going over the ridge into areas where there might be some friendly personnel stationed. Inaccurate fire of that sort constituted an artillery incident requiring an official investigation. Nervous subordinate officers convinced the new major that he did not want to account voluntarily for unintended accidents. He agreed that they should wait to find out if there had been any casualties of friendly fire before getting involved, and the group concluded that they had not seen anything that might incriminate their unit. Sounds familiar, doesn't it?

CAMP TOWNES CHAPEL

In the spring of 1967, the 4/60th Artillery Unit moved from the Phu Cat Airbase to Camp Townes near Qui Nhon. In time, the unit improved one of the tent covered wooden frame buildings into a tin roofed chapel. With a coat of paint, the chapel served the compound nicely.

CHAPEL ON THE HILL CAMP TOWNES

By the end of their first year in Vietnam (January, 1968), the men of the 4/60th Artillery had built a fancy chapel on a hilltop in the center of the Camp Townes compound. Green and gold colored glass panes were used to make a large decorative window behind the altar in the shape of a cross.

GOING HOME

Every soldier who served in Vietnam knew a precise date he was scheduled to complete his combat tour and return to "the world" (home in the United States). My year was programmed to end on Feb. 12, 1968, and I kept track of the time to serve in country by counting the number of Sundays ahead of me before I could depart. The troops constantly bantered with each other about how much time they had left to serve. The less time you had remaining on your tour of duty, the more status one had. Rather than competing with each other regarding who had seniority by date of rank (who got promoted first over whom), the "Date of Expected Rotation Overseas" (DEROS) was the supreme arbitrator of who was who in Viet Nam. Usually a soldier did not start gloating about being a so-called "short-timer" until they were within 100 days or less of leaving.

So when the troops began comparing their low rotation day numbers with each other, I would mislead them by saying I only had forty-something workdays left. This made me seem like one of the low boys in the crowd, until I smiled and bragged that chaplains only worked on Sundays. When I really did get close to going home, I joined in the fun by mirthfully teasing some junior officers in our unit. If they had longer to serve than me, then I would comment that they must have committed some awful crime to be sentenced to so much time in Vietnam. The poor guys would moan that the hardships of Vietnam included having a heartless chaplain who ribbed others about being a short-timer, especially long suffering souls like themselves. Their feigned pleas for mercy made the teasing even funnier. I probably should serve a little extra time in purgatory for joining in the fun a bit too gleefully back then.

To celebrate and illustrate their official countdown to departure, some of the men made calendars to mark off each day remaining, counting down from D-100 to Departure Day. The calendars often took the shape of artistic figures that were colored in by the numbers until the whole picture was shaded on the very last day. The most popular design was a playboy type centerfold with the low day numbers centered on the most private parts of the model (if you get my drift). Of course, I would seemingly disapprove of the nudity, while asking if their picture was supposed to be of Eve in the Garden of Eden. To my credit, I never posted a short-timer's calendar in my "hooch" (living area). Some soldiers think it is only because I couldn't draw. But if I had made a countdown calendar, I would have used a picture of the great silver freedom bird (an airplane) that would eventually take me home to dear ol' El Paso.

The lighthearted repartee about DEROS masked the anxious fear troops felt in their last days in Vietnam about something bad happening to them right before they were scheduled to leave for home. If you get killed, maybe it doesn't matter when it happens; except nobody wants to die on the last day before hostilities are to end for him or her. Morale suffered terribly when we received a report about someone who was killed during his short-timer's period before departure. Consequently, a lot of the men got very, very careful about surviving the war the closer they got to their rotation date. The ultimate precaution would have been to live the final weeks in a sandbag bunker and have your meals brought to you, until it was time to dash for the nearest airfield—then fly quickly to the out-processing center at Cam Ranh Bay. Men who were not short-timers would taunt the departing soldiers about the frequency of helicopter and plane crashes occurring while traveling around the country, especially lately on the routes to you-know-where.

While riding the circuit in my jeep about nine months into my tour of duty, I noticed that one jeep driver of mine was feeling spooky about the unescorted trips we were making into the backcountry to visit remote troop positions. The dangers were no greater than usual, but the young trooper was quite nervous about being ambushed while passing through the peasant filled villages, or the ominous prospects of mines being planted overnight in the primitive dusty rutted roads. I had forgotten that he was one of the draftees who finished his two years of conscripted service while in Vietnam. Hence, he did not have to finish a full twelve months in combat like most soldiers. You should never make fun of anyone's fears, but I had to insist that we make the usual trips into the countryside. The driver was reluctant to ride with someone who had long since conceded that any day could be his last one, going where we were going. The man's replacement arrived early, and he was greatly relieved to spend the last days of his tour in the seemingly safer environment of the well-guarded Fourth Infantry Division Headquarters base camp in Pleiku.

During the last thirty days before rotating back home, I kept my regular active schedule of long road trips, seeing troops and saying goodbye to all. I felt rather proud of myself for trudging onward, when the temptation was to slow down my visitations and "stack arms," as the old timers would say. Whenever armed troops are on a training break, they take their rifles and hook them up with each other in a self-supporting stack, using swivels affixed near the end of the rifle muzzle. When a soldier was going to take it easy, he might say that he was stacking his arms, or that he had stacking swivels on his belt so he could lean in a stack and do nothing like the rifles.

While feeling self-satisfied about not slacking off at the end of my tour, my driver took us down beautiful, palm tree lined Highway One from Qui Nhon to Nha Trang. The road took us around the sides of seaside mountains with breathtaking views of the azure warm waters of the South China Sea. If we drove near the edge of the switchback roads traversing the mountainside, I could scc the beaches below the cliffs that bounded the side of our bumpy road. We were alone on a steep mountain curve when I spied a round, smoking, dark metal object about 100 meters ahead of us. I ordered the driver to stop immediately, because there was the danger of a grenade waiting for us. We waited with trepidation to see if the object would explode. The mysterious ball continued to emit white vapors for at least five minutes before I had the driver cautiously creep the jeep forward to examine what kind of booby trap was blocking our passage. The grenade turned out to be a large motor transmission bearing that must have bounced off the underside of a recent transportation truck. My driver and I laughed at ourselves while driving past the "bomb," and finished our journey, making jokes about having bravely avoided a dangerous truck part.

When the Viet Cong launched the Tet Offensive in late January of 1968, our unit fought in the most intense battles of my tour. As soon as I could get cleared for travel, I rushed to the sites where our men had blasted back the streaming hordes of doped up VC and NVA attackers. Assured that the men were safe, we commented about how this sensational action had occurred when we were within two weeks of leaving. I speculated that the high command might extend our tours and freeze our departures, at least until they were more certain of the course of events. To my pleasant surprise the S-1 (adjutant and personnel officer) issued orders for me to leave Viet Nam on 7 FEB 68, five days less than a full year's tour. Most troops counted on getting a few days dropped from their official departure dates, and sure enough I had gotten mine in the midst of a countrywide crisis. The battalion sent me to Cam Ranh Bay, some two days before departure, to participate in the out-processing routines and to have a few nights off-duty in a very comfortable setting. Before leaving the unit headquarters, there was a farewell party for the large group of us who had been in the unit since its start up training at Fort Bliss. Because we had shipped out together, and were leaving together, the group was called "the hard corps who were going home." I composed a poem for the occasion that commemorated by name the men we had known and grown to love in our year on foreign soil. After every verse, the troops drank a rambunctious toast.

The thirsty celebrants shouted for more and more of my eloquent, whiz-bang rhyming passages as the evening progressed. By the time the party ended, I could have gotten an ovation for reciting the alphabet.

In my last days at Camp Townes, Vietnam, I observed the sentimental leave-taking rituals that signal you are finally going home. There is no more precious thought then knowing you are going to be reunited with your beloved family after a year's absence. The day I had desired so longingly was at hand, and my excitement grew with every preparation I made to leave. I packed my footlocker and duffle bag with a few meager possessions and simple souvenirs. The starched khakis that were to be worn on the plane back to the states were carefully laid out, for proudly pinning on the campaign ribbons I had earned for serving in Southeast Asia. My black fatigue belt buckle was left as a welcoming present for the chaplain who would replace me in the 4/60 Artillery. A few troops came by to shake my hand, saying goodbye with the hope we might see each other somewhere, sometime, in the years to come. One Cajun noncommissioned officer reassured me about our prospects of meeting again with an old French proverb that says: "Only the mountains never meet." I was glad to leave Vietnam, yet sad to leave the men I had come to know so well. My driver put my gear in the back of the jeep, and drove me to the flight operations building at the Qui Nhon airport. I napped away the hours of waiting for a plane by leaning on my duffle bag, keenly listening for a space available passenger call for any military mission heading toward Cam Ranh Bay. I remember to this day hearing some popular music sung by The Supremes being played on a loud speaker, reminding me that I was returning to "the World."

The flight to Cam Ranh Bay was an hour-long "short hop" into a well-developed Army compound on the sandy hills of a natural deep-water port. The Americans had selected Cam Rahn Bay to be one of its major logistical support and replacement depots for the war effort. The base was so secure that the troops who processed in and out of this base believed it had never been attacked. The out-processing personnel did everything within their power to make us feel safe, so we could begin to relax as part of the transition back home. The service club had live entertainment each evening for troop diversion and amusement. We turned in our faded, worn out, jungle fatigues to the supply section, then quickly changed into our stateside khakis for the last few hours before departure. Next, we exchanged our military pay currency for U.S. currency, legally allowing us to carry greenbacks once again. A cadre of officers flying out the next day had a farewell party the evening before the long awaited departure. That last night in Vietnam on 6 FEB 68, may have been one of the happiest nights of my entire life. The lighthearted party was truly one of the very last acts before loading on a plane to go home the next day. My buddies bought each other round after round of bar drinks, sang any and every song that the volunteer pianist could remember, while praising each other's military exploits – namely that all had survived and were unharmed. We exchanged information about our next assignments in hopes of keeping in contact with each other, knowing we were about to be we scattered to the widespread stateside Army bases awaiting us. Men who have been in combat with each other develop an unparalleled closeness that lasts a lifetime. I love those men, and the memories of serving together with them, more and more with every passing year.

Some of us slept fitfully, waiting for the wake-up call that signaled our departure day had finally begun. Others had slept heavily, perhaps because of over sedating themselves at the going home party. A few celebrants had gotten up during the night to visit the latrine, occasionally to "toss their cookies" (alcohol is known to irritate the hardiest of stomachs). We were hastily assembled in a pre-flight area where our luggage was to be inspected for contraband. The Military Police warned the prospective passengers about the penalties for smuggling—especially live ammunition, grenades, and captured weapons prized as war souvenirs. After being given repeated opportunities to dispose of illegal materials, officers were shown deferential treatment and exempted from the final luggage search on the pretense that there was not sufficient time left to open the bags before boarding. The military hired commercial airlines to haul troops in and out of Vietnam. These civilian crews wanted to off-load the new arrivals, refuel, and have the departing people get on board as quickly as possible to minimize the plane's time in the war zone. So, literally, you could have one group of men coming off the plane passing by another group of out-bound men waiting to take their seats. On one such occasion, a vainly ignorant departing soldier told a newly arriving trooper, that in life, some people win and some people lose; and that the newly arrived man was a loser. The observation, while true, was also cruel. The Vietnam War was, in one way or another, torturous for all of us; creating unresolved bitterness for some who served there.

The long eighteen-hour flight home had to stop in Japan for re-fueling. We then flew to Guam, being allowed for the first time to disembark the plane and shop in the air terminal PX. While there, I bought a genuine Mikimoto pearl necklace to give my wife upon our reunion. The flight stopped again for re-fueling on Midway Island, where it was nighttime in their time zone. We were reversing the time zones, while flying eastward, making it difficult to calculate how long the trip was lasting. The on-board sound system had music channels for us to enjoy with individual headsets that helped pass the time. Somehow we found out from a news broadcast that the North Koreans had just captured the USNS Pueblo, and were holding the crew as hostages. This international crisis reminded us about the perils men in uniform face daily, and we identified with those helpless sailors immediately. The mood was somber throughout the flight, and would have been regardless of the latest developments abroad.

As we made a midnight landing in Seattle, Washington, the passengers gave the pilot a rousing round of applause for one of the most perfect landings I've ever enjoyed. I had expected that the men might spontaneously begin cheering to celebrate being back in America, but that did not happen; nor was it the mood one felt when we quickly exited the plane, and sought to make connecting flights to our homes across the nation. Before rushing off to my departure gate, I gave Lieutenant James Miller a souvenir to remember the unexpectedly close relationship we had developed in Vietnam and had commemorated while flying home. He was reminded that he might have saved my life with his good advice about how to travel on mine filled roads. I took the Chaplain's cross off my shirt collar, pressed it into his hand as we shook hands goodbye, and prayed that we might see each other again in the years ahead. The first leg of my journey home took me through the Los Angeles Airport. Doc Anhalt accompanied me on this late night flight, since his home was in Bakersfield, California. He had been my best friend in Vietnam, and has remained in contact with me every year since then. We parted company with an embrace as he met his wife to go home to his precious family, leaving me to wait for my connecting flight to Texas. Sleepy fatigue induced to nap against my Army duffle bag while I spent four or five long hours laying over in the L.A. Air Terminal before my final morning flight to El Paso. The family was eagerly waiting for me that bright, clear February morning to joyfully welcome me back home, ending the longest year of my life. As I kissed my wife and hugged our children, Bobby and Jeannie, I secretly promised never to be away from them again.

GOING HOME
DEROS

Celebrating their last night in Vietnam on 6 FEB 1968, at the Cam Rahn Bay Officers Club, seated around the table from left to right, were an unidentified celebrant in fatigues, CPT Bill Law, LT Grant Sehr, LT Zigurd Berzins, LT Harold Hein, LT James P. Miller, and CPT "Doc" James Anhalt. DEROS means Date Expected Rotation from OverSeas, which for this group was 7 FEB 68.

FREEDOM BIRD

The long awaited flight back home to America
was known as the freedom bird back to "the
world." Commercial aircraft were hired to
rotate troops from stateside and back again at
the Cam Rahn Bay depot. Despite the cloudy
day and the rain showers, everyone leaving wore
sunny smiles.

AS LONG
AS I LIVE

When I was in country, I promised myself in front of several chapel members that I would never overly sentimentalize my wartime experiences in Viet Nam. There would be no return trips in later years to view the places where I had traveled to commemorate battles or dramatic events. This military venture was not like World War II with its sacred beaches at Normandy and Iwo Jima, worthy of pilgrimages and memorial services. The troops in Nam just wanted to serve their twelve months and go home, as if they had put in a long day at the office and were back from work on their own time. Three decades later, I have come to appreciate that some men and a few women have needed to go back to the places of their ordeals and traumas, in order to resolve the conflicts in their hearts and minds. In some cases, the trips have been acts of reconciliation with a former enemy. So far, my interests and needs have not required that I book a flight to Ho Chi Minh City, formerly ol' Saigon. But I, too, was permanently affected by the time I spent in jungle fatigues on foreign soil in harm's way, and in some unexpected little ways as well as the obvious ones.

I still get very melancholy whenever I hear Scott McKenzie sing, "Are you going to San Francisco?" His song was highly popular before my unit shipped out, and I thought about the lyrics when our troop ship sailed out from the Oakland Military Terminal under the Golden Gate Bridge. When I heard it played again while overseas, I would become very home sick. Once while on R&R in Bangkok, I heard a Thai female vocalist sing this song at an officers club. I was so affected by the music that I wanted to hear an encore, but my friend, Chaplain Swede Erickson, USAF, wisely dissuaded me from walking up to the stage to make my request. The song is stuck in my head because of Vietnam.

When a movie about Vietnam comes to town, I usually try to see it in hopes that somebody will finally tell our story the real way we lived it. Burt Lancaster produced and starred in my favorite cinematic portrayal of the war. **Go Tell The Spartans** got it right when it came to describing the MAC-V advisors phase of the campaign. Unfortunately, this film was an independent production, not getting wide release nor doing much box office business. Another factual movie that captured part of the war experience was **Hamburger Hill**. The infantry, as usual, bore the brunt of the casualties as this movie bloodily documents. As it goes nowadays, my interests have also centered on reading a few paperback war novels if they are authored by a Vietnam veteran like Don Rast. Otherwise, I am not too interested in the opinions of outsiders; and I absolutely cannot bear to watch a movie starring Jane Fonda.

After arriving home, I craved fresh milk more than any other foodstuff, since it was never available in Vietnam. I love real ice cream too. Fresh eggs are still a breakfast treat after gagging on powdered eggs loaded with monosodium glutamate for a year. Real chocolate, that doesn't contain cellulose to keep it from melting in the tropical heat, will never be taken for granted either. I still chuckle about the time I spent trying to redeem some disposable coke bottles on my first weekend stateside. The war had created a gap in my familiarity with American product development that made me feel embarrassingly ignorant and behind the times.

On a more serious note, I sometimes cringe at the sound of unexpected gunshots. For example, when I was on R&R in Honolulu, my wife and I went shopping at a department store to buy some gifts for her to bring home to our children in El Paso. Over in the toy department, a child played with a machine gun replica that fired a series of semi-realistic gunshots. I literally had to stop myself from hitting the floor to take cover. Gunshots never used to bother me before Vietnam. Firing a weapon, or being around firing lines, is still perfectly fine. But sudden and unseen shooting, or loud noises that sound like gunfire, get on my nerves to this day.

When beginning my journey to Vietnam, I expected to learn something about my inner fears. Most soldiers want to be brave, and are afraid they might let their buddies down. Before shipping out, I discovered how much I was suppressing these anxieties by experiencing some transient somatic reactions. My nervousness subsided by the time we arrived in Vietnam. You can acclimate to many things for the sake of survival. The surprising self-discovery was about my hidden aggressions. My partisanship grew rapidly in the midst of trying to stay alive while supporting the people around me. You quickly lose objectivity in battle, and it took great self-restraint to remain a noncombatant as my chaplain's role required. If I had been authorized to bear arms in a different capacity, I came to realize how enthusiastically the guns would have been put to active use.

Throughout my year away from home, I reflected deeply about the consequences of missing so much of my children's development. I sent them letters and souvenirs to compensate for being an absentee father; but this was not the same thing as tucking them in bed at night after reading them a story, or playing tickle games to please them. Maybe they did okay without me that year, but I did not do okay without them. I always remember the small tape-recorded messages my wife and I exchanged through the mail so we could hear each other's voices. The military is full of unaccompanied separations that are hard on a family man like myself. Defending families is what motivates people to serve in the military. Family life is what makes us want to be civilians instead of full time career soldiers. If the national security is in danger, then I will sign up again to defend our borders; otherwise I plan to stay home since I already gave at the office on one occasion. Vietnam convinced me to be a citizen soldier and follow a reserve unit career, rather than pursue a twenty-year active duty retirement with its many attendant benefits.

As much as I cared about my own family life, I genuinely grieved about the tragic effects the war wrought upon the Vietnamese people. Many a time, while riding through tiny villages, I watched the poor peasants working in the fields or their small shops, and imagined how they must view having to endure one more set of foreigners in the land. I fantasized about the collection of national flags they hid in the huts that might be used to salute the "Army of the Day" who passed their way. The war torn civilians may have had their personal political convictions, but survival had meant the necessity of accommodating themselves to the Japanese, the French, the South Vietnamese Government, the Viet Cong, and the Americans with their allies. Upon returning to the safety of my own homeland, I watched the poignant accounts of the boat people struggling to escape to a better life, and wanted to find a way to help them. I occasionally offered to sponsor refugee families, having always felt a tie with the Vietnamese who have settled in America when I meet them in daily life. As a soldier who once lived with them, I enjoy having them live among us now in the United States. Would you care to join me for lunch at my favorite Vietnamese food restaurant sometime?

Most of all, when I reverently visit a Vietnam War memorial monument and a veterans' counselor shakes my hand while telling me "welcome home," my eyes well up with tears for finally being accepted for who we were and where we went. Vietnam veterans were shunned when it mattered, and consequently, our unassimilated return remains as some serious unfinished business. As many veterans are fond of saying, "the war may be over, but not in my head." Most didn't want a parade, or a medal, or fancy speeches upon their return –just respect. We just wanted a little appreciation for what we had done in uniform. Many bearing "the marks" of war have discovered that it is up to us to help each other recover from Vietnam, or it won't get done at all.

To all of you who returned safely, I thank God for this return and am grateful for your brotherhood. As for our fallen comrades in arms, I pray that God is keeping their souls close by His side until we can answer roll call together in that great kingdom to come. Like every generation who has ever been sent into combat, I sincerely pray that God will bless America with everlasting peace, and lament that our successors must accrue war stories of their own.

In the words of the prophet:

> *"May the Lord judge between the nations, and arbitrate for many peoples; so that they shall beat their swords into plowshares, and their spears into pruning hooks, and neither shall they learn war any more"* (Isaiah 2:4). Amen.

THE NATIVE
COMES HOME

Staying a year in Vietnam has an effect on a man. You absorb many influences while adapting to a new place that has strong, exotic new culture. Some men went native while away from home. Coming home was a process of re-acclamation to peace time, civilian living. But going home was always the objective.

THE ACCIDENTAL CAREER

My service as a military chaplain occurred because of an unexpected and unlikely series of events, proving that the good Lord works in many mysterious ways. He evidently has quite a sense of humor about our inherent human weaknesses too. Theoretically, none of my military experiences should have ever taken place, much less a tour in Vietnam. If my parents had not conspired to keep me at home for enrollment in a local college, I might never have worn an Army uniform. Mom and Dad had sought to keep me from ever voluntarily enlisting in any branch of the military. Dad had been drafted in World War II at age thirty-five, though happily married and the father of two children. Accordingly, I had been warned repeatedly about the folly of becoming a soldier. But paradoxically, since I was parentally steered toward admission to Trinity University in San Antonio, I became obligated to enroll in the school's mandatory ROTC for all male students in my freshman and sophomore years. The irony of these events escaped me then; but not now, when I can look back, contemplating how God has forged my destiny.

Once enrolled in ROTC for two years, the Professor of Military Science and Tactics successfully indoctrinated me into believing the best way to avoid the draft board, in order to stay in college, was to sign a contract to continue enrollment in ROTC through my junior and senior years to earn a reserve lieutenant's commission. The Trinity ROTC cadre's motto was that if you were going to serve in the military, then a graduate ought to be an officer rather than an enlisted person.

Besides gaining a draft deferment, the ROTC contract had the additional benefit of paying us ninety-cents a day. The monthly stipend provided me with date money (movies cost fifty cents in those days, and I was very active socially). Sometimes, I wondered if I had sold out my birthright like Essau once did for some meat-red pottage (soup) when he was starving for food, and was thus exploited by his twin brother Jacob (Genesis 25:29-34). But America was in a Post-Korean War period of peace and contentment under President Eisenhower, and besides that, I had no specific plans for the future. Being in the Army was a good way to spend my time compared to anything else I could think of doing with a mathematics degree. Besides, there were high expectations of being sent to Germany, where I envisioned owning a red Chevrolet Corvette, while dating the buxom German girls like so many other carousing soldiers had done. How naïve can a twenty-one year old guy be?

Upon my college graduation day of 30 May 1960, I was commissioned a second lieutenant in the Army Artillery Corps. In those days, Army ROTC graduates usually served just six months on active duty, spending the rest of their time in reserve units or the standby reserve (the option I hoped to be assigned). Some of us were given a two-year active duty assignment (oops, I did), and a few others were offered a regular army commission, having a minimum of three years service (which I declined). After being notified of my prospective tour assignments, the good Lord intervened, reminding me that I had been called to the ministry and should enroll in seminary immediately after graduation. My college cheerleading buddy, and lifelong friend, Swede Erickson, had forged my name on a letter requesting application forms from a seminary. He was going to The Perkins School of Theology at Southern Methodist University, and thought that I should be going with him. Swede correctly perceived that I was avoiding a religious vocational calling that had come to me at a summer church camp while in high school. When the application forms arrived at my parent's house, Swede admitted his complicity in the ruse, and validly urged me to surrender to the army of the Lord. Who says that God must always speak from a "burning bush" when He calls us?

Admission into the Perkins School of Theology at Southern Methodist University (SMU) in Dallas deferred and delayed my active duty service obligation to the Army, but it also complicated things. The Army transferred me out of the Artillery Corps into the Staff Specialist Corps (a holding group for officers in professional or graduate school.) The kicker was, that as a clergyman, I would be draft exempt and might not be subject to military service at all. A Trinity classmate and ROTC graduate, who also went to seminary at SMU a few years ahead of me (Will Schaefer), said he had simply ignored his officer's commission. The Army somehow forgot about his military obligation. That did not happen to me. During my three years of theological training, I regularly got Army newsletters offering to place me in an active reserve unit, but without pay (the rules for Chaplains were somewhat different than for other officers.) After graduation and ordination, my status remained a second lieutenant Staff Specialist, until I gained several years of civilian pastoral experience. Pastoral parish experience was a Methodist requirement to be approved for endorsement as a military chaplain within our denomination. Without church approval, the Army could not transfer me into the Chaplains Corps. Administratively, the Army could only retain me in the VIII CORPS Reserve (holding) Group without pay or promotion. I stayed in this "limbo" category from May 1960 to January 1966.

There are very few Army officers who have remained a second lieutenant for five and one-half years in grade; especially, since all of my ROTC contemporaries on active duty had gotten promoted to first lieutenant after two years. During the height of the Vietnam War, the promotions from second to first lieutenant were accelerated, coming after only one-year in-grade. Once again, the career that I had never expected, much less ever wanted, didn't show much promise for the future, until good ol' Vietnam came along.

It was the fall of 1965, when over confident U.S. forces in Vietnam were undergoing a rapid buildup, chided onward by a few early victories. The Methodist Church was allowed a quota of fifty new Army chaplains, so I got invited to go to active duty. I had ulterior motives for leaving the nice little rural church in Stockdale, Texas, where I had been serving for eighteen months. Officer's pay with my entering rank of first lieutenant was much more than I was earning as a civilian pastor. The G.I. Bill educational benefits would pay for the graduate training I eventually wanted to get in counseling psychology. The prospects of travel and varied experiences were attractive too. My period of service was for a minimum of three years. The Chaplains Corps had an 80% retention rate even during wartime because of the multiple benefits afforded officers (other officer branches were as low as 20% in their retention rates during Vietnam). I was clear about my desire and need for specialized graduate training, and announced beforehand, that when I completed my service obligation I would get discharged and return to civilian life.

True to personal convictions, upon returning from Vietnam to the USA, I planned to legally end my military career at Ft. Hood, Texas, on 30 May 1969. I made preparations for moving to Austin, to begin graduate school studies at the University of Texas, where I had been accepted for doctoral studies. Once again, the Lord providentially brought more career counseling into my life through a local Methodist pastor in Killeen, who had befriended me while stationed at Fort Hood. I had confided to him about some plans to work as an Associate Pastor for a local Methodist church in Austin, while using the G.I. bill to support my pregnant wife and two children as I worked on my advanced degree. The pastoral friend casually suggested I shouldn't resign my officer's commission just yet, but stay in the Army Reserve to earn extra money that would defray increased expenses of civilian life ahead of me. Sure enough, there was a reserve engineer unit in Austin, Texas, with a vacancy for a chaplain. The Lord does not have to beat me over the head with the Tableau of the Ten Commandments to get my attention. I signed up to remain in the Army Reserves.

Joining the 871st Engineer Army Reserve unit could just have been a short-term means to a professional goal. Never did I consider myself to be a "lifer," the derogatory term draftees used for people who had voluntarily stayed in the Army. This insinuation was that "such people" were pursuing the Army as a life's vocation, maybe because they couldn't make it in the real world. Despite having some nine full years military since originally being commissioned, I had not accepted the identity of being a career man. Thus, when leaving active duty I didn't mind having to start all over again in my tenure as a captain, even though I had already held the rank for three years on active duty. The next promotion, from captain to major in the reserve forces, would take another seven years. At that same time the active duty officers who were captains were getting promoted to major in only two to three years. Counting my active duty and reserve periods of service, I wore the rank of captain for ten years, another inauspicious harbinger for career prospects. But I did not see further military service in my future, since I thought my reserve Army time would end when I got my Ph.D.

You might already anticipate what happened when I earned my degree. Yep, another Army friend got my attention by pointing out that at age thirty-four, I had earned thirteen years longevity in the Army, with seven good years vested in retirement benefits. He rhetorically asked if I had any other investments or other retirement programs besides social security. Knowing full well that I had made no such provisions, he advocated that I stay longer in the reserves until I completed enough time for eventual retirement benefits. This was the moment of truth when I became a "lifer," even though I kidded myself into thinking that I would stay in the reserves on a year-to-year basis to help pay off a few debts accrued while going to graduate school. After getting promoted to major and then to lieutenant colonel, I met the minimum officer requirements for retirement. I announced that I was finally leaving the military, after achieving my mandatory removal date with twenty-eight years of being an officer. With only three months left in my career, I got one last promotion to full "bird" colonel that extended my service two more years. Advancement to this rank surprised me, because only eleven percent of the chaplains had gotten this promotion; and it was the only way I would have agreed to any further service. Somebody up there not only liked me, but had further need for me to continue serving as a military chaplain in the Texas Army National Guard.

Retrospectively, I realize that God provided me with thirty fulfilling years of public service as an Army chaplain that was perfectly suited to my interests and abilities. I loved the ecumenical collaboration among the clergy of different faiths, and cherished the access to the cross-cultural, international, multi-racial personnel in uniform. My special interest in pastoral counseling was grandly fulfilled by the countless troops with problems needing personal assistance who continuously came to my attention. I am truly grateful for all of the so-called accidents that got me started and kept me in uniform through the years. Maybe I should have paid for this honor and privilege, but instead I made a good living getting to do good in the Lord's name. How blessed can one man be?

FOR GOD
AND COUNTRY

The Chaplains Corps needs clergy men and
women of all faiths to serve God and country in
war and peace.

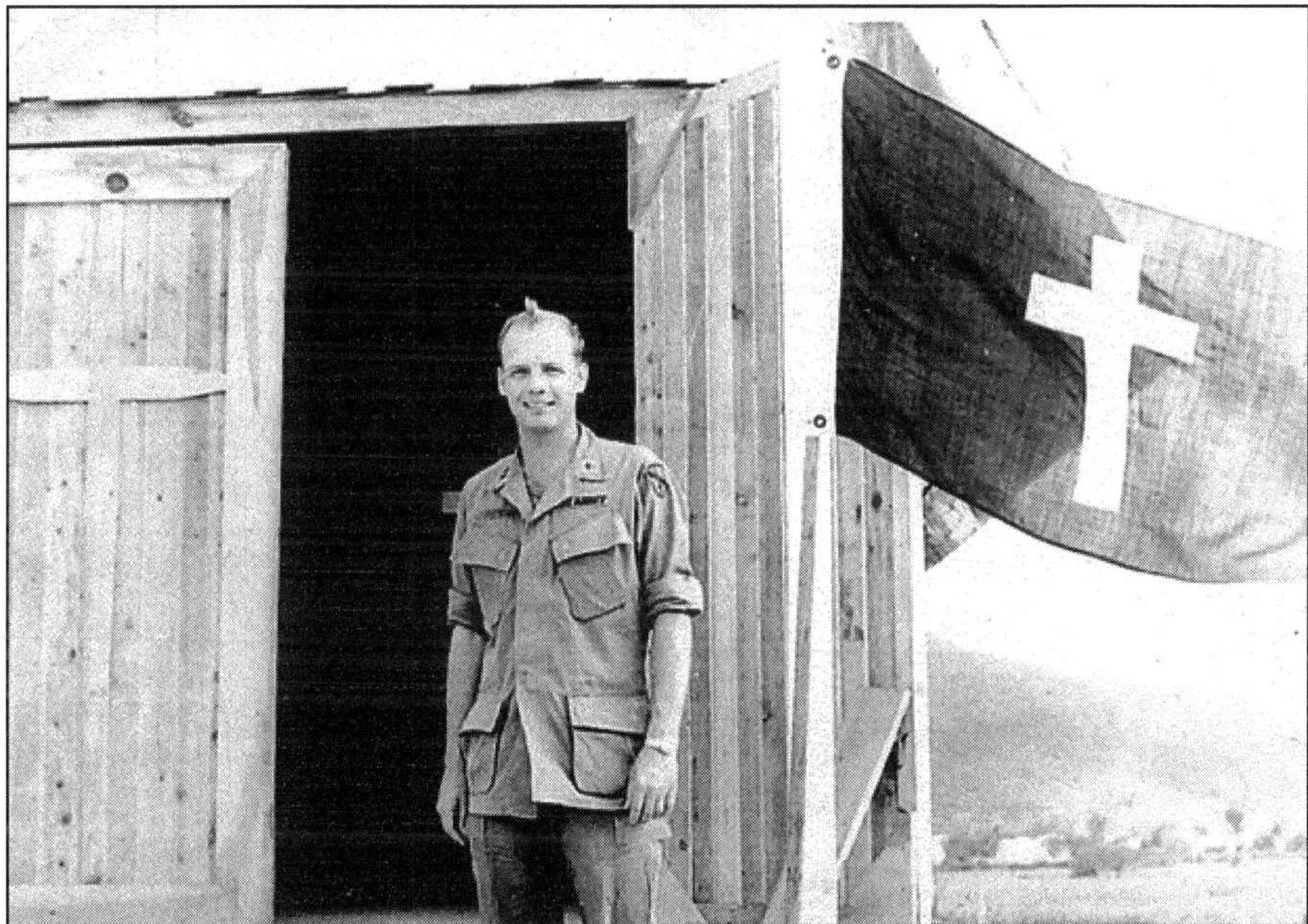

A FINAL REMEMBRANCE

Recently, I was jogging around the Army parade grounds at Fort Sam Houston in San Antonio, Texas, about 5:30 PM, when I heard the sprightly bugle call of "retreat' that signals the lowering of the American flag in front of the post headquarters. The cannon fired and the ceremony began. A southerly breeze ensured the colors were fully unfurled, as they were gently brought down the tall staff that was clearly visible from my slow moving perspective. As military custom required, I stopped and stood at attention, saluting the national emblem until it was recovered by the honor guard. Then a tear crept into my eyes and uncontrollably rolled down my cheek, when remembering the sacrifices and hardships that military personnel have incurred in the service of that flag. The ceremony was completed, and the joggers resumed their rounds, getting fit to defend the very flag we had just respected. And I was there with them again, remembering.

Remembering is the watchword for many veterans. In 1985 a number of my former Army buddies felt the need to remember all those, living and deceased, who paid the price of military service in Air Defense Artillery units between 1965-73 in Vietnam. They formed a veterans network, holding annual reunions to honor the dead, and support those who can't forget what they saw and did. On Veterans Day 2000, in Washington D.C., I attended my first reunion with the men of the Dusters, Quads, and Searchlights, (DQS) Veterans Association. After thirty-two years separation, I was deeply gratified to see the soldiers I had once known when we had been young men on a misguided mission in Southeast Asia. We stayed up late reliving our combat experiences, and catching up on what has happened since then. One hundred of us trooped past the names of our fallen comrades listed on the Vietnam Memorial. We laid three wreaths in their honor and cried again while tracing their names on paper from the marble tableaus. One of our veterans, Joe Belardo, lovingly placed his hands on a group of Army and Marine names whom had fallen together during a pitched battle so long ago, yet so fresh and real in his grieving mind. How can we ever forget their sacrifices while we are still alive? During the war years of 1965-73, a total of 184 men from our combined units died in Vietnam. That evening, we reverently called the roll of their names and lit up flashlights for each of the departed as part of the association's annual act of remembrance. The solemn occasion inspired me to compose a few lines of poetry to commemorate our laying wreaths at the Vietnam memorial.

The old soldiers stepped slowly and softly,
To set a heartfelt wreath
Before The Wall's roll of war's wrath,
Lamenting their lost youth and youths lost.

During our veterans reunion our group hosted and honored the Gold Star Mothers who had lost sons in Vietnam. We hugged and consoled them in hopes we could fill their family voids in some surrogate way. The DQS association has begun to raise funds to send some of these mothers on escorted trips to Vietnam, if they desire to see where their boys had fought and died. I have offered to contribute proceeds from the publication of my writings to sponsor some of these trips hereafter. It would be a privilege to go along with them, if they need someone to carry their suitcases or steer them around the back roads we once traveled. Vietnam has changed since we were there, and so have we. The story once lived has not ended, but continues onward. And that is how it should be. Life goes on, and we can too if we place our faith in God and promise to love each other more dearly in the days still allotted to us.

Shalom.

A FINAL
REMEMBRANCE

The old soldiers stepped slowly and softly,
To set a heart felt wreath,
Before The Wall's roll of war's wrath,
Lamenting their lost youth and youths lost.

APPENDIX: OPERATION GOLD STAR

- If you are interested in supporting the Operation Gold Star (OGS) program that sends American Gold Star Mothers to Vietnam where they can resolve their losses of sons and daughters, please send your donations to:

    Mr. Clyde Larsen, DQS/OGS Treasurer
    353 Dartmouth
    Elgin, Il 60123

- For information about Operation Gold Star, please check the OGS web site:

    www.operationgoldstar.org

- You may communicate with organizational officers if you desire information about OGS. Please contact:

    Mr. Ed Allen at (812) 845-2303
    DusterEd@juno.com

    Mr. Joe Bellardo at (908) 754-5129
    dusterman@erols.com

- Written correspondence may be sent to:

    National Dusters, Quads, & Searchlights Association
    P. O. Box 198
    Cynthiana, IN 47612-0198

May God bless your generosity for this and all other charities that you support.

ABOUT THE
AUTHOR

Samuel W. Hopkins, Jr. was born in San Antonio, Texas, where he completed Edison High School, and graduated from Trinity University with a B.S. degree in mathematics. As a distinguished military graduate of the ROTC, he was commissioned as a second lieutenant in the U.S. Army Reserve before enrolling in the Perkins School of Theology at Southern Methodist University in Dallas, Texas. He earned a Master of Theology degree and was ordained as a United Methodist minister. After serving two civilian pastorates, he was placed on active duty and served in Vietnam as the Chaplain of the 4th Battalion 60th Artillery. He returned to reserve duty status and enrolled in graduate studies at the University of Texas at Austin, earning his Ph.D. in counseling psychology. He completed his military career in units of the Army Reserve and the Texas Army National Guard. Chaplain Hopkins advanced to the rank of Colonel before his military retirement after 30 years service, having been decorated repeatedly for his meritorious performance of duty.

In his extensive civilian career as a licensed psychologist, Dr. Hopkins was ecclesiastically appointed to serve in the mental health programs of state psychiatric hospitals and state prisons. Within these agencies he became an acclaimed program director and department head. His broad experience also includes provision of services in private hospitals, clinics, and nursing homes. His academic interests led him to teach graduate school for the University of Southern Mississippi, publish professional articles, and make frequent presentations at training conferences.

Sam married Patsy Ruth Hopkins in 1964, he enjoys having three children and six grandchildren. His interests include playing tennis, riding on 50 mile bicycle tours, listening to Celtic music, collecting Irish stamps, writing movie reviews, and visiting with friends. As time and budget permit, he loves foreign travel, in or out of uniform, as attested in his remembrances of Vietnam.

PHOTO INDEX

www.ingramcontent.com/pod-product-compliance
Lightning Source LLC
Chambersburg PA
CBHW080455110426
42742CB00017B/2894